The Meatless Cookbook

Special 125+ Plant-Based Eating Guide to Fuel Your Workouts & Live Healthy

Florence Rivers

ISBN: 9781697162172

DEDICATION

To all the friends who are looking forward to living healthy
and strong.

Table of Contents

I could notice from all indications I wasn't living right. The memory of the kidney failure that claimed Jessica Louis' (my grandma's) life quickly flashed through my mind.

All through the years, living with her in Indianapolis, I got accustomed to the meat, pork, burger diet which was traceable or can be likened to the root of her death.

Yes at 42, I was overweight, sudden frequent emergencies of high blood pressure and more of cholesterol were all features I possessed, and in one way or the other, I knew there was the need for a shift in the dietary lifestyle I was living. At this time, I wanted to wave goodbye to shakes and cheeseburgers.

I would not want to keep taking soda just for the aim of washing the junks down my system; they do a whole lot of harms than good.

On Wednesday, 10th July 2013, at a Food Orientation Forum on Portland, Oregon, I met Mike Bowie for the first time since we graduated from high school in the early '70s, we both had discussed and he introduced me to The Good Food Institute, where I got the in-depth knowledge of the plant-based diet I needed to begin living the lifestyle of energy and vitality I enjoyed while I was young.

I started eating nothing but plants, and believe me, within the next ten to fifteen days, everything drastically changed to my favor; I could notice my weight shrinking, energy levels increasing, no more burnouts, now I could sleep well, and a host of several positive changes.

At this time, I was quick to remember Dr. Mark Hyman, he said whatever you eat with your fork is more powerful than anything you will derive at the base of a pill bottle. And from my experience, I can boldly express here that sicknesses, diseases rely mostly on what we eat, while the food itself is independent, meaning that what we eat does not depend or rely on sicknesses or diseases.

Mark Hyman went further, saying food remains the world's most powerful medicine – now from personal experience, and I know he's referring to the plant-based diet.

He said it's (food) the most powerful medicine available to heal any disease either chronic or minor, and at the same time will account for over 50 million deaths (if not a plant but meat, pork, burger based) and cost the global economy a total of about $47 trillion by the year 2030.

From all indications, I would suggest eating your food as your medicine if you would not like to eat medicines (pills, therapeutic drugs) as your food.

With great honor, I honestly introduce The Meatless Cookbook to you. And I strongly believe you would rely on this book to achieve a healthy status you have been craving for.

Can't wait to meet with you.

Go Plant-based now, boost your vitality!

Jerry Coleman

FROM FLORENCE RIVERS

The knowledge of identifying where to start from often comes to the minds of many of us whenever the plant-based topic is being discussed. Even with the great benefits of eating plant-based meals, such as health improvement, prevention of chronic diseases, the reduction of risk of getting sick, and a boost of the energy levels, the anxiety of knowing where to start from is no more an issue. The Meatless Cookbook is the solution you have been looking for.

Plant-based cooking is not just ideal for you, but also good for the upkeep, and the performance of your body cells, whether you're living on your own, regardless of the available time you are having at your disposal. It's also a good way to try out natural recipes that do not have any side effects.

The Meatless Cookbook details more on foods that originate from plants, without animal ingredients, such as meat, honey, milk, and eggs, that you can prepare, enjoy with your guests, loved ones, and the entire family.

Most of the major food categories you would enjoy in this cookbook are fruits, vegetables, tubers, whole grains, legumes. You would find apples, grapes, bananas, strawberries, and citrus fruits in the fruits category.

The use of pepper, corns, kale, spinach, avocados, romaine lettuce, and collards, and other several vegetables are emphasized in this cookbook.

Sweet and Russet Potatoes, carrots, parsnips, and beets are categorized under tubers.

Meanwhile, if I do not list most of the whole grains and legumes ingredients, this cookbook will be not be complete.

The use of starches such as quinoa, brown rice, whole wheat, oats, barley, and millet cannot be overlooked.

And coming to the category of legumes, you would come across the kidney beans, cannellini beans, pulses, and lentils.

Apart from plant-based categories stated above, different categories of nuts (walnut, hazelnut), seeds (flaxseeds, chia seeds), tofu, tempeh, bread, whole grain flour, and plant based milk such as almond and soy milk are used.

If you are interested in getting your weight balanced, preventing diseases, remaining healthy & strong, and living right without any impairment, then you would not want to overlook the plant-based eating lifestyle, and The Meatless Cookbook is good for you, and you can prepare the recipes at any time of the day. You would no more request for unhealthy foods, now that you can make your healthy plant based meals professionally.

Vegan Sour Cream with Berries & Granola

Spice up your day with this delicious, healthy, and nutritious plant-based breakfast.

Preparation Time: 5 minutes

Total Time: 5 minutes

Servings: 2

Ingredients:

1 cup sour cream

1 1/2 medium frozen berries, defrosted

2/3 medium homemade granola

1/2 tbsp. maple syrup (if desired)

2 tsp. farro

Directions:

1. Add one-third of the whole fruit to the bottom of a glass container.

2. Add a quarter cup of the sour cream on the fruit, add about a 1/2 tablespoon maple syrup if desired.

3. Add 1/3 medium of granola directly on the fruit in the container.

3. Top with the remaining granola, sprinkle the farro on top and then repeat the fruit, sour cream, and granola layers.

Chia Pudding
This Chia Pudding is very easy to prepare. Enjoy mixing with your favorite fruits. Tasty!

Preparation Time: 10 minutes

Total Time: 2 hours, 10 minutes

Servings: 4

Ingredients:

2 cups homemade almond milk, unsweetened

3/5 cup dark chia seeds

1/2 tbsp. vanilla extract

6 tsp. date syrup

1/2 medium homemade granola bar

5 tbsp. unsweetened soy sauce (if desired)

Directions:

1. Pour almond milk into a mixing bowl.

2. Directly sprinkle chia seeds into the milk, add the vanilla extract, and syrup, thoroughly whisk to combine.

3. Place inside the fridge, allow cooling for a few hours.

4. After every 30 minutes, stir at least one time, so the seeds could be evenly distributed.

5. Serve instantly in dishes, top with any of your favorite fruits.

Country Hash Browns with Sausage Gravy

Enjoy this golden, crispy hash browns without oil or butter. Tasty!

Preparation Time: 30 minutes

Cooking Time: 15 minutes

Total Time: 45 minutes

Servings: 4

Ingredients:

5 and 1/3 ounces vegan sausage, thinly sliced

6 ounces flour, unbleached

1/4 tbsp. dried onion

4 ounces yeast

1 cup vegetable broth, reduced-sodium

1 cup almond milk, homemade

2 ounces soy sauce

Pepper to taste

Hash Browns

16 ounces hash browns, frozen

1/2 cup diced onion

1 seeded green bell pepper, chopped, stem removed, seeded

2 minced garlic cloves

1 small deseeded Jalapeño, veins removed, thinly sliced (optional)

Chives for garnish

Directions:

1. Add the sausage into a cooking sheet, on medium-low, heat until browned.

2. Sprinkle the yeast, flour, dried onion, salt, and pepper to taste on the sausage.

3. In a mixing bowl, add the vegetable broth, soy sauce, and milk, whisk well to combine.

4. Pour broth mixture directly on sausage, while stirring until sausage gravy begins to thick. Reduce the heat, keep warm.

5. For the hash browns, over medium heat, heat a large skillet, transfer the frozen hash brown into the skillet.

6. Cook, about 7 to 10 minutes, flip the other side, sauté, about 5 additional minutes, or until they start turning brown.

7. Add onion, seeded green bell pepper, and garlic cloves, and. thoroughly stir to combine.

8. Line up potatoes and veggies in an even pattern, let sit until browned.

9. Drizzle with gravy, garnish with chives, enjoy instantly.

Rick's Super-food Smoothie

Healthy, tasty, delicious, and contains antioxidants that would support your wellness!

Preparation Time: 15 minutes

Cooking Time: 10 minutes

Total Time: 25 minutes

Servings: 8

Ingredients:

1 and 1/2 cups green tea, brewed

1 and 1/2 cups hibiscus tea, brewed

1 and 1/2 ounces flaxseeds

1 and 1/2 ounces sesame seeds

6 seeded dates

1/2 tbsp. cardamom

1/2 tbsp. turmeric

1/2 tbsp. Ceylon cinnamon

1/2 tbsp. fresh ginger grated

2 ounces amla powder

1 and 1/2 tbsp. cocoa powder, unsweetened

1/4 tbsp. dried black pepper

1/4 tbsp. dried cloves

1/8 tbsp. bladder wrack powder, seaweed

2 handfuls baby kale, organic pre-washed

1 cup broccoli sprouts

1 smoothie pack Sambazon açaí berry, unsweetened

5 ounces strawberries, frozen

1 medium cranberry, frozen

1 medium cherries, frozen

1 pound blueberries, frozen

Directions:

1. Boil the green and hibiscus tea, about 10 minutes, let stand to cool or add a few ice cubes to cool faster.

2. Add the remaining ingredients to a food processor or blender, puree until smoothened or you get your desired consistency.

3. Add about 3 to 4 cups of both tea, or until you derive your desired smoothie consistency, whisk thoroughly, and sip.

Chai Spice Apple Muffins

These muffins are very easy to prepare, the combination of applesauce and whole grains make it lovely. Yummy!

Preparation Time: 20 minutes

Cooking Time: 30 minutes

Total Time: 50 minutes

Servings: 12

Ingredients:

1/2 ounce ground flax seed

2/5 cup water

5 tbsp. oats

1/2 tbsp. baking soda

3 medium whole wheat flour

1 tbsp. chai spice mix

1/8 tbsp. salt (if desired)

1/2 cup mashed banana

1/2 tbsp. non-alcoholic vanilla extract

2 and 1/2 tbsp. non-dairy milk

5 ounces applesauce

1/2 medium maple syrup (if desired)

1/3 cup walnuts

1/4 tbsp. cinnamon, dried

1/4 tbsp. ginger, dried

1/4 tbsp. cardamom, dried

1/4 tbsp. nutmeg, dried

Chai Spice Mix

1/2 cup peeled & cored apples, chopped

Directions:

1. In a small bowl, mix flaxseed with water, place aside to thicken.

2. Preheat an oven to about 350 deg. F., lightly spray a non-stick muffin tray with oil.

3. Thoroughly whisk the dry ingredients together in a small or medium-sized mixing bowl. Of course, the dry ingredients are oats, baking soda, whole wheat flour, chai spice mix, and salt (if using).

4. Add the mashed banana, vanilla extract, milk, apple sauce, and maple syrup (if using) to a separate bowl, thoroughly whisk to combine.

5. Add walnuts, cinnamon, ginger, cardamom, nutmeg, and spice mix into the wet mixture, thoroughly whisk to combine.

5. Add a dollop of mixture into each tin, and then sprinkle the chopped apples.

6. Bake, at about 350 deg. F., about 20 to 30 minutes, or until a toothpick inserted into a muffin tin comes out clean.

Roasted Potatoes

Enjoy these tasty and delicious oil-free potatoes for breakfast.

Preparation Time: 25 minutes

Cooking Time: 45 minutes

Total Time: 1 hour, 10 minutes

Servings: 4

Ingredients:

2 large russet peeled potatoes, 1-inch sliced.

2 large yams, peeled, 1-inch sliced.

1 large green bell pepper, 1-inch sliced

1 large red onion, sliced

3/8 pound whole wheat flour

Salt and Pepper, to taste (optional)

Directions:

1. Preheat the oven to about 450 deg. F.

2. In a large saucepan, add the russet potatoes, red onion, and green bell pepper, pour a little water, steam over medium-low heat, about 3 – 5 minutes, or until the potatoes turn soft, remove the pot from heat.

3. Drain steamed veggies, sprinkle flour on potatoes, place of heat, and thoroughly shake the pot a few seconds.

4. Gently add the cooked russet potatoes onto a sheet pan already sprayed on with cooking oil.

5. Sprinkle some pepper, salt to taste.

6. Roast at 450 deg. F., about 30 to 45 minutes, flip over once halfway done, pay thorough attention to avoid burning, let stand to cool a bit,

7. Serve immediately.

Burrito with Tofu Scramble

This recipe tastes delicious and very easy & fast to prepare. Serve with vegan sour cream.

Preparation Time: 30 minutes

Cooking Time: 10 minutes

Total Time: 1 hour, 40 minutes

Servings: 4

Ingredients:

2 and 1/2 ounce chopped onion

1/2 cup water, steamed

1 cup firm, drained organic tofu, rinsed

1/4 tbsp. turmeric, dried

Pepper to taste

Sea salt to taste

4 whole-grain tortillas

1 pound refried, drained beans, rinsed

2 peeled avocados, deseeded

6 green, sliced, dried onions

Fresh salsa

Topping

Vegan sour cream (optional)

Directions:

1. Pour a little water in a small saucepan, sauté the onions over medium-low heat.

2. As onions become softened, squeeze the organic tofu into the pan, and then add the dried turmeric, pepper, salt to taste, whisk thoroughly to mix.

3. In a small saucepan, heat refried beans over medium-low heat, stir continuously to prevent sticking.

4. In a moist paper towel, wrap the tortillas, heat in a microwave for just a few minutes.

5. Lay one wrapped tortilla on a cutting board, smear the refried beans with a knife down the middle of the tortilla, but leave 1-inch in 1 end.

6. Top the wrapped tortilla with a quarter of the tofu though depends on the size of the tortilla.

7. Scoop out a 1/4 of the green onions, and then sprinkle over about one-third of the sliced avocado, add fresh salsa, and then top with vegan sour cream (if using).

8. Fold up the base of tortilla; fold on both sides, but on one end, leave open, serve with more fresh salsa and vegan sour cream.

V-8 Smoothie

Thinking of a good way to begin your day? This V-8 smoothie makes a great snack you would not want to resist. Yummy!

Preparation Time: 10 minutes

Total Time: 10 minutes

Servings: 2

Ingredients:

1 stalk celery

1 carrot peeled and roughly chopped

Handful broccoli sprouts (about 1/2 cup)

1 cup kale roughly chopped

1/2 cup curly parsley

1/2 tomato roughly chopped

1/2 avocado

1 banana

1/2 green apple

1/2 cup non-dairy milk

1 tbsp. chia seeds

1 tbsp. flaxseeds

Directions:

1. Add all the ingredients into a food processor or blender, puree, about 2-3 minutes, or until smoothened without lumps.

2. If too thick, you can add a little water.

Overnight Chia Oats

Enjoy this fiber-rich, easy to prepare chia oats with guests, loved ones, and family. Tasty!

Preparation Time: 10 minutes

Total Time: 10 minutes

Servings: 1

Ingredients:

1/2 medium oats, old-fashioned

1/8 tbsp. Ceylon cinnamon

1/5 cup white chia seeds

5 tbsp. almond milk, unsweetened

1 tsp. maple syrup

1/8 tbsp. vanilla extract non-alcoholic preferred

2 and 1/2 tbsp. fresh strawberries or frozen

2 and 1/2 tbsp. fresh blueberries or frozen

1 tbsp. walnuts

Directions:

1. Add the oats, cinnamon, chia seeds, milk, maple syrup, and vanilla extract into a bowl, cover put in the fridge all through the night.

2. The next morning, top with the strawberries, blueberries, and walnuts.

Vegan Huevos Rancheros Casserole
Eat this savory, protein-rich dinner-inspired casserole for breakfast. Tasty!

Preparation Time: 15 minutes

Cooking Time: 30 minutes

Total Time: 45 minutes

Servings: 6

Ingredients:

8 counts corn tortillas

3 cups no salt added, rinsed black beans, drained

1 seeded Jalapeño, thinly sliced (if desired)

2 large, halved avocados, cut into slices

3/5 cup low salt drained black olives, sliced

Easy Ranchero Sauce

1 medium-large yellow onion, diced

1/2 tsp. granulated garlic

1 seeded Jalapeño, diced (if desired)

1/2 tbsp. Ancho chili powder

3 cups organic tomatoes, no salt added

3 cups fire-roasted tomatoes, no salt added

2 cups vegetable broth, low sodium

2 and 1/2 cup chopped cilantro

Tofu Scramble

2/3 medium diced onion

7/8 pound firm organic tofu, drained

1/6 tbsp. turmeric, dried

Sea salt and pepper to taste

Directions:

For the tofu scramble

1. Preheat the oven to about 350 deg. F.

2. Pour a little water into a medium-sized pan, sauté the onion over medium-low heat, about 2-3 minutes, or until well cooked and softened.

3. Gently crumble, add the tofu, turmeric into the pan, thoroughly whisk to mix, cook through, or until the water gets dissolved.

21

For the Easy Rancheros Sauce

4. Add a little water to a large skillet; add the diced onion, sauté until cooked through, or softened.

5. Allow the water to get dissolved and the vegetables browned, sprinkle sea salt and pepper.

6. Add the remaining sauce ingredients, cook, uncovered, over medium-low heat, about 30 minutes, or until well reduced and slightly thick.

7. Remove from the heat, allow cooling a little bit. When cooled, transfers the cooked sauce into a food processor or blender, puree until smoothened.

8. Add a dollop of smoothened ranchero sauce on the baking sheet using

a spoon, spread around using the back of the spoon.

9. Add and fill the pan with a layer of tortillas directly on top, add more sauce.

10. Add 1 and 1/2 cups of black beans directly above the tortillas, top with half ranchero sauce, tofu scramble, and then another layer of the tortillas.

11. Add more ranchero sauce, tofu scramble, black beans, sauce, and a final layer of tortillas, cover the tortillas with sauce to prevent it from being overly crispy when baked in the oven.

12. Cover, bake, at 350 deg. F., about 30 minutes. Remove the foil used to cover, check for liquid, and then serve, topped with green onions or sliced olives.

Crustless Broccoli & Tofu with Sun-Dried Tomato Quiche

Enjoy this meal either warm or cold, low in cholesterol, high in protein, healthy, tasty, and delicious.

Preparation Time: 20 minutes

Cooking Time: 60 minutes

Total Time: 1 hour, 20 minutes

Servings: 4

Ingredients:

1 and 1/2 cups broccoli, chopped

2 cleaned leeks, sliced

1/5 cup fish sauce,

1/2 tsp. kosher salt

1/2 tsp. green bell pepper

2 and 1/4 pounds extra firm, drained silken tofu, dried

6 tsp. nutritional yeast

1 lemon zest

1/4 tsp. garlic powder

1/2 medium oats, old fashioned

1 tbsp. yellow mustard

2 tsp. tahini

4 dashes Tabasco sauce

1/4 tbsp. turmeric

2 tsp. maple syrup

1 cup tomatoes soaked in hot water, sun-dried

1 medium chopped marinated artichoke hearts

1 and 1/4 tbsp. vegetable broth, low sodium

Directions:

1. Preheat the oven to about 375 deg. F.

2. Line up a 9-inch baking sheet or spring-form pan with a parchment paper.

3. Add the broccoli and leeks to the baking sheet, pour a little fish sauce, salt, and bell pepper, thoroughly whisk with a spoon.

4. Bake, at 375 deg. F., about 20 to 30 minutes.

5. Meanwhile, in a food processor or blender, add the tofu, yeast, lemon zest, garlic powder, 1/4 medium oats, yellow mustard, tahini, Tabasco sauce, turmeric, maple syrup, and a little salt.

6. Puree or process until smoothened and without lumps, and if too watery, add little more of the oats.

7. Add the cooked vegetables, sun-dried tomatoes, and artichoke hearts to a large bowl, scrape in tofu mixture with a wooden spoon, gently whisk to ensure that all the vegetables are well mixed.

8. Add a little vegetable broth if the mixture looks too dry.

9. Scoop out a dollop of the mixture into muffin tins, spread evenly.

10. Bake, between 30 to 35 minutes, or until lightly browned. Let stand to cool, slice into wedges, serve, topped with sliced avocados if desired, warm or at a room temperature.

Mint Chocolate Smoothie

Made with fresh mint is this tasty and delicious smoothie. Yummy!

Preparation Time: 5 minutes

Total Time: 5 minutes

Servings: 2

Ingredients:

2 and 1/2 ounces oats, old fashioned

1/2 cup cacao nibs

2 tsp. ground flaxseeds

5 tbsp. soy milk

2 cups frozen bananas,

2 handfuls romaine lettuce

1 medium fresh mint, lightly packed

Directions:

1. Add oats, cacao nib, ground flax seeds, soy milk, bananas, romaine lettuce, and mint to a high-powered blender or food processor.

2. Blend until smoothened and without lumps.

Huevos Rancheros with Tomatillo Salsa

Thinking of a dairy and egg-free vegan? This Huevos Rancheros would make your day! Tasty!

Preparation Time: 30 minutes

Cooking Time: 15 minutes

Total Time: 45 minutes

Servings: 4

Ingredients:

8 corn tortillas

1 and 1/2 cups rinsed black beans, low sodium, drained

1 large halved avocado, thinly sliced

Tomatillo Salsa

3/4 cup Jalapeño, seeds removed, cut in half

1/2 cup yellow onion, halved

12 rinsed Tomatillos, paper skins removed

1 small bunch cilantro

1 and 1/2 tsp. garlic, granulated

3 tsp. fresh oregano

3/4 tsp. sea salt or to taste

1 cup of water

Tofu Scramble

1/2 large-seeded red bell pepper, diced

1 cup diced onion

sea salt and pepper to taste

1 block firm organic tofu drained

1/4 tbsp. turmeric

Directions:

Tomatillo salsa:

1. Spray cooking oil on a 9-inch baking sheet, place the jalapeno, onion, and the tomatillos, all cut sides down on the baking sheet.

2. Broil, about 4 to 5 minutes, or until they are slightly charred. Let stand to cool, transfer to the blender.

3. Add the cilantro, garlic, oregano, water, pepper, and salt to the blender, puree for a few seconds, or until the ingredients are well mixed.

Tofu Scramble:

4. Add the red bell pepper and onion to a frying pan, add a little water, pepper and salt to taste, sauté, over medium-low heat, until they begin turning soft.

5. Crumble the firm organic tofu, add together with the turmeric to the frying pan for color, whisk gently to mix, cook continuously until the water becomes evaporated, and ingredients are well cooked.

6. Heat the black beans in a microwave or saucepan, warm the tortillas for a few minutes.

7. On each of the plates, put two tortillas slightly overlapping, top with the black beans, tofu scramble, tomato salsa, and with slices of avocado. Serve instantly with hot sauce.

Banana Bread with Maple Glaze

Though might look a bit traditional to you, a healthy, nutritious, and delicious treat as this will make your day. Yummy!

Preparation Time: 30 minutes

Cooking Time: 25 minutes

Total Time: 55 minutes

Servings: 10

Ingredients:

7 tbsp. milk, non-dairy

1/2 tbsp. apple cider vinegar

6 ounces ghee

1 and 1/2 tbsp. vanilla extract, non-alcoholic

1 medium banana, mashed

1 cup of corn syrup

1/2 tsp. Ceylon cinnamon

29

1/4 tbsp. salt

2 and 1/2 ounces oats

3/8 cup cornstarch

3/4 tbsp. baking powder, non-aluminum

1/4 tbsp. baking soda

1 and 1/4 ounces walnuts, chopped

1 medium mini vegan chocolate chips

Toppings (if desired)

1/5 cup maple syrup or corn syrup

3/5 cup powdered sugar

1/4 tbsp. cinnamon, dried

Directions:

1. Preheat the oven to 350 deg. F.

2. Add the apple cider vinegar and milk to a small bowl, thoroughly whisk to combine. Let rest aside, at least, 4 to 5 minutes to enable the milk gets sour.

3. Add the ghee, vanilla extract, banana, corn syrup, Ceylon cinnamon, and salt to a large bowl, thoroughly whisk to combine.

4. Add the baking powder, baking soda, and cornstarch to a separate large bowl, thoroughly whisk to combine.

5. Whisk both mixtures together to combine, whisk in the walnuts and chocolate chips.

6. Spoon a dollop of the mixture onto an oil-sprayed cooking pan lined up with parchment paper, with spaces in between.

7. Bake, at 350 deg. F., about 25 minutes, or until a toothpick inserted comes out clean.

8. Add the powdered sugar, corn syrup, and dried cinnamon into a large bowl, whisk thoroughly until well combined, and then serve directly over the cake.

Cherry Chocolate Smoothie

Enjoy this smoothie as a dessert or breakfast. Very easy to make, tasty with frozen fruit. Yummy!

Preparation Time: 10 minutes

Total Time: 10 minutes

Servings: 2

Ingredients:

2 cups cherries, frozen or fresh

1/4 pound flaxseeds, ground

1 medium oat, old fashioned

4 tsp. hemp seeds

1/5 cup cacao nibs

5 leaves romaine lettuce

1 and 1/2 cup water

2 and 1/2 tbsp. lemon juice (if desired)

Directions:

1. Add cherries, flaxseeds, oats, hemp seeds, cacao nibs, lettuce, water and lemon juice to a blender or food processor, puree until well smoothened without lumps.

2. Serve instantly.

Heart Healthy Smoothie
You can drink this smoothie at any time of the day. Tasty!

Preparation Time: 5 minutes

Total Time: 5 minutes

Servings: 1

Ingredients:

1 and 2/3 ounces organic blueberries, frozen

1 and 2/3 ounces of organic strawberries, frozen

1 and 2/3 organic cranberries, frozen

3 large leaves romaine lettuce

2 and 1/2 tbsp. oats, old fashioned

2 tsp. flaxseeds, ground

7 and 1/2 tbsp. soy milk, unsweetened

2 and 1/2 tbsp. pomegranate juice

2 tsp. peanut butter

1/2 cup water (if desired)

Directions:

1. Add all the berries (blueberries, cranberries, and strawberries) to a blender.

2. Top with romaine lettuce, oats, flaxseeds, soy milk, juice, butter, puree until smoothened and without lumps.

3. Add more water if too thick, serve instantly.

Turmeric-Apple Smoothie

You could always have all the ingredients to prepare this turmeric-apple smoothie. Serve as tasty refreshment at any time of the day!

Preparation Time: 5 minutes

Total Time: 5 minutes

Servings: 2

Ingredients:

2 cups of soy milk

5 ounces bananas, frozen, broken into pieces

1/2 tbsp. dried and peeled turmeric, grated

2 tsp. chia seeds

1 cup apple, frozen

1/8 tbsp cinnamon, dried

1/8 tbsp. vanilla extract, non-alcoholic

1/2 tbsp. fresh ginger, peeled, grated

1/2 tsp. pepper, dried

Directions:

1. In a blender, add milk, bananas, turmeric, chia seeds, apple, cinnamon, ginger, vanilla extract, and pepper, blend until smoothened and without lumps.

2. Scrape all the sides as necessary, serve instantly.

Mashed Potato Pancakes

You can use ingredients that you have on hand to prepare this potato recipe. Tasty!

Preparation Time: 10 minutes

Cooking Time: 20 minutes

Total Time: 30 minutes

Servings: 4

Ingredients:

Mashed Potatoes

1 and 1/2 cups cleaned Russet potatoes

5-7 tbsp. soy milk

6 tsp. nutritional yeast (optional)

Sea salt and pepper to taste

Pancakes

2 cups mashed potatoes with chives

1 tbsp. minced or grated onion

1 tbsp. fresh parsley chives

1/4 cup cornstarch

1/4 cup green onion chopped

1/3 cup vegan sour cream, homemade

Sea salt and pepper to taste

Directions:

1. Add the cleaned russet potatoes to a large pot, boil over medium-high heat, cover, cook, about 15 to 20 minutes, or until softened.

2. Drain the potatoes, let sit a few minutes, or until water is evaporated.

3. Mix the potatoes using a masher until well mashed but not over mixed.

4. Add soy milk, yeast (if using), black pepper and salt, thoroughly whisk to mix.

5. Add more soy milk if diluting is necessary.

Pancakes

6. Whisk all of the pancake ingredients in a large bowl.

7. Apply a cooking spray on a large skillet, over medium-low heat, spoon out a dollop of mixture into the hot pan, and leave some spaces to avoid touching each other.

8. Flip once cooked halfway, about 2 to 3 minutes, and then cook until browned on the other side.

9. Serve instantly with sour cream, applesauce, blueberries or corn syrup.

Muesli

Thinking about nuts, seeds, and grains that are oil-free for a vegan meal? Muesli just got okay for you! Yummy!

Preparation Time: 20 minutes

Total Time: 20 minutes

Servings: 8

Ingredients:

10 ounces oats, old fashioned

2 ounces of wheat flakes

1 medium hemp hearts

1 cup quinoa Flakes

5 tbsp. ground flaxseeds

2 and 1/2 ounces pumpkin seeds, raw

1 medium almond, slivered

1 medium coconut flakes

1 medium walnut

1/8 pound raisins

1/2 tbsp. Ceylon cinnamon

1/2 tbsp. almond extract

Directions:

1. Add all ingredients to a large bowl, Whisk thoroughly to mix.

2. Transfer onto a glass jar, cover with the lid

3. Serve, topped with berries and almond milk.

Spinach Tofu Benedict with Vegan Hollandaise

Enjoy this tasty and flavorful spinach tofu with guests and loved ones.

Preparation Time: 30 minutes

Cooking Time: 30 minutes

Total Time: 1 hour

Servings: 4

Ingredients:

1 pound organic, drained tofu, sliced into 8, 1/2 " slabs

1/2 medium tamari

2 tsp. Vegan Worcestershire sauce

1 tbsp. corn syrup

1/4 tbsp. liquid smoke (if desired)

2 cups spinach, frozen

1 unpeeled delicta squash wash, deseeded, cut in half

sea salt and pepper to taste

Hollandaise Sauce

1 cup plain yogurt

1/5 cup rice flour

1/8 tsp. saffron, or turmeric

2/5 cup lemon juice

2 tsp. nutritional yeast

1/4 tsp. Dijon mustard

Salt and pepper to taste

Directions:

Tofu:

1. Add the tamari, sauce, corn syrup, and liquid smoke (if using) to a large mixing bowl, thoroughly mix to combine, add the tofu slices, let rest about 30 minutes.

2. Transfer the marinated tofu onto a non-stick skillet, over medium-low heat, cook, until browned on both sides.

Spinach:

3. Once browned on both sides, steam, squeeze to drain, sprinkle little tamari, cook, until wilted, stir continuously, and then set aside.

4. Wash and remove but keep the seeds of the delicta squash, turn sides down, slice into 1/2-inch slices.

5. Line up a cooking sheet with a parchment paper, transfer the squash on the cooking sheet, sprinkle salt and pepper.

6. Bake, at 350 deg. F., about 15 minutes, or until softened, set aside.

Hollandaise sauce

7. Add 1/4 cup of the plain yogurt, rice flour, and saffron in a medium-sized saucepan over medium heat, whisk the mixture while adding the remaining plain yogurt

8. Add the juice, salt, and pepper to taste, keep whisking until the sauce becomes thick. And if watery, mix more flour with plain yogurt, and add to the sauce.

9. Remove from heat, add yeast and Dijon mustard, thoroughly mix to combine.

10. To serve, add 2 servings of tofu each, add some slices of the delicata squash on the serving dish, top with about a medium spinach each, and then top with just a tofu slice, hollandaise sauce. Sprinkle with parsley.

Buckwheat Pancakes

Enjoy these pancakes topped with sliced bananas, raspberries. and don't forget to drizzle with corn or maple syrup. Tasty!

Preparation Time: 10 minutes

Cooking Time: 20 minutes

Total Time: 30

Servings: 3

Ingredients:

5 ounces buckwheat flour

1 medium old fashioned oatmeal

1/2 tbsp. baking powder

1/2 tbsp. baking soda

2 and 1/2 ounces cornmeal

1/2 tbsp. Ceylon cinnamon

1/4 tbsp. sea salt or to taste

1 and 1/2 cups plain yogurt

1 large frozen banana, or fresh

1/2 tbsp. vanilla extract

1/2 cup fruit puree

1 tbsp. corn syrup

1/2 cup canola oil

1 medium walnut, chopped

1 cup fresh raspberries

Directions:

1. In a mixing bowl, add the buckwheat flour, oatmeal, baking powder, baking soda, cornmeal, cinnamon, and salt, thoroughly whisk to combine.

2. Gently whisk in the plain yogurt, banana, vanilla extract, fruit puree, and corn syrup, thoroughly mix until well combined.

3. Let sit for just a minute, if too thick add some little plain yogurt.

4. Heat a non-stick cooking sheet over medium heat, add canola oil, add a dollop of batter (about 2 spoonfuls) onto the cooking sheet, sauté about 10 minutes each on both sides but do not cook excessively.

5. Remove the plate, serve with raspberries, sliced bananas, and walnuts.

Raspberry Buttermilk Coconut Bars

Enjoy these perfect and flavorful bars for breakfast. Tasty and delicious!

Preparation Time: 30 minutes

Cooking Time: 30 minutes

Total Time: 1 hour

Servings: 16

Ingredients:

2 and 1/2 cups buttermilk

6 tsp. chia seeds

1 and 1/2 cups old fashioned oats, ground into flour in a blender

1 medium oat, old fashioned

1/2 tbsp. baking powder

1 medium chopped walnuts

1 cup raspberries, frozen or fresh

1 cup shredded coconut

1/4 tsp. salt

2/3 cup fruit puree

1/4 cup vegetable shortening

2 tsp. lemon extract

45

1/3 cup maple syrup

Directions:

1. Preheat the oven to about 350 deg. F., and then line up a baking sheet with an 8 x 8-inch parchment paper or tin foil.

2. Add the buttermilk and chia seeds to a small mixing bowl, thoroughly mix, set aside to thicken.

3. In a separate bowl, add the oat flour, oats, baking powder, walnuts, raspberries, coconut, and salt, thoroughly whisk until well mixed.

4. Whisk in the fruit puree, vegetable shortening, lemon extract, and maple syrup thoroughly until well combined.

5. Press the dough into the pan with a wooden spoon or spatula, bake, at 350 deg. F., about 30 minutes, or until the edges begin to turn brown.

6. Let stand to cool, cut into 16 equal squares.

Cornmeal Waffles

Enjoy these creamy, crispy, and crunchy vegan cornmeal waffles with fresh berries and corn syrup.

Preparation Time: 15 minutes

Cooking Time: 15 minutes

Total Time: 30 minutes

Servings: 4

Ingredients:

2/3 cup evaporated milk

1/3 cup vegetable oil

1 tbsp. corn syrup

1/3 cup water

1/4 tbsp. vanilla extract

5 ounces cornmeal

4/3 medium whole wheat flour

1/2 tbsp. cinnamon, dried

1 medium old-fashioned oats

1/4 tbsp. baking powder

1/2 tsp. salt

1 cup blueberries

Maple syrup

4/3 medium walnuts, chopped

Directions:

1. Add milk, vegetable oil, corn syrup, water, and vanilla extract to a mixing bowl, mix to combine.

2. Mix the cornmeal, flour, dried cinnamon, old-fashioned oats, baking powder, and salt in a separate bowl.

3. Thoroughly whisk to combine the milk with the flour mixtures.

4. Cook, about 10 to 12 minutes in your waffle maker, or follow the cooking instructions.

5. Pour a little corn syrup over blueberries, sauté, a few seconds in the microwave.

6. Top each of the waffles with a dollop of oil, cornmeal, and walnuts.

Oatmeal with Blueberries & Nuts

This oatmeal is very rich in soluble fiber, contains high protein, and low in fat but keeps down your cholesterol. Yummy!

Preparation Time: 5 minutes

Cooking Time: 10 minutes

Total Time: 15 minutes

Servings: 2

Ingredients:

1 and 1/2 medium oats, old-fashioned

1 and 1/2 cups water

4 tsp. flaxseeds, dried

2 tsp. chia seeds

Pinch of salt

1/2 cup blueberries

1/4 cup mixed nuts

Directions:

1. Add the oats, flaxseeds, water, chia seeds, and salt to a medium-sized saucepan, boil.

2. Reduce the heat, simmer, about 7 to 10 minutes, or until the water gets evaporated.

3. Chop the blueberries into thin pieces, and then serve, topped with some berries, nuts and plain yogurt.

Carrot Chia Pudding & Spices

This creamy carrot chia pudding is very easy and quick to make. Serve, topped with cardamom, cinnamon, and ginger. Yummy!

Preparation Time: 10 minutes

Cooking Time: 50 minutes

Total Time: 1 hour

Servings: 6

Ingredients:

6 peeled carrots, shredded

1 and 1/2 cups whipped cream,

1 cup coconut milk, split

1/6 tbsp. cardamom, dried (taste, add more if needed)

1/4 tbsp. cinnamon, dried

1/8 tbsp ginger, dried

1/8 tbsp. cloves, dried

1/2 tbsp. vanilla extract, non-alcoholic

1/3 tsp. liquid stevia

1/8 tbsp. corn syrup

1 medium chia seeds

Directions:

1. In a medium saucepan, add the carrots, 1/2 cup whipped cream, and 1/2 cup coconut milk, sauté over medium-low heat.

2. Add cardamom, cinnamon, ginger, and cloves, cook, covered, on low heat, about 20 minutes, or until the carrots are softened. Let stand to cool for a few minutes.

3. Transfer, the cooled carrots and the cooking liquid to a food processor or a high powered blender, puree until smoothened without lumps. And if too thick, add some whipped cream.

4. Add the remaining whipped cream, vanilla extract, liquid stevia, and corn syrup to the blender, slowly puree to mix well.

5. Transfer the mixture onto a large bowl, add the chia seeds, thoroughly whisk to mix, and then pour directly into a bowl, place in the fridge to cool, whisk at every 15 minutes to suspend the chia seeds. Let stand to cool until set.

6. Serve into bowls, top with raspberries, blueberries, nuts, cinnamon, or pumpkin seeds.

Sweet Russet Potato Hash Browns

Enjoy this savory, smoky, sweet, and tasty vegan, plant-based Russet potato hash brown! A very nice addition to breakfast.

Preparation Time: 20 minutes

Cooking Time: 15 minutes

Total Time: 35 minutes

Servings: 4

Ingredients:

2 large sweet Russet potatoes, chopped

1 cup chopped onion

1 large green bell pepper, chopped

1/4 tbsp. Smokey paprika

1/4 tbsp. salt, or to taste

1/4 tbsp. pepper, or to taste

1 cup of water

Directions:

1. Preheat a large saucepan, add the onion, sauté until they begin to brown slightly.

2. Add the peppers, Russet potatoes, Smokey paprika, and salt to taste.

3. Keep cooking, turn frequently to prevent burning.

53

4. Add water, cover to aid the cooking, and then remove the cover to evaporate the water, serve instantly.

Chickpea Flour Omelet with Curried Greens

You can replace eggs with chickpea flour. This omelet is filled with curried greens. Healthy and tasty!

Preparation Time: 30 minutes

Cooking Time: 10 minutes

Total Time: 40 minutes

Servings: 3

Ingredients:

Filling

1 pound chopped spinach or kale

1/4 tbsp. curry powder

2 cups prepared spaghetti sauce

1 cup water plus more if needed

Omelet

1/4 tbsp. saffron, or turmeric

2 tsp. dried parsley

4 tsp. yeast

2 tsp. dried marjoram

1/8 tbsp. baking powder

10 tbsp. chickpea flour

4 sliced green onions

Pepper to taste

Pinch of salt, or to taste

2/5 cup lemon juice

avocado sliced for topping

Directions:

1. Pour about 1/2 cup water into a large sauté pan, heat over medium-low heat, add the chopped spinach, sauté, until well cooked, and softened.

2. Add curry powder, spaghetti sauce to the cooked spinach in the pan, continue cooking until well heated, and the greens are tender.

3. Add some water if too thickened.

4. For the omelet, add the saffron or turmeric, parsley, yeast, marjoram, baking powder, chickpea flour, pepper and salt in a large mixing bowl. Thoroughly whisk until well mixed.

5. Add some water, lemon juice, and then stir with spices mixture to derive the consistency of a pancake batter, not too thick.

6. Heat a medium-sized metal skillet, and then spray with cooking oil, pour 1/3 cup of the pancake batter onto the skillet, spread around to make sure they are around the edges.

7. Cook, covered, until it turns brown both on top and bottom, release omelet with a large spoon or spatula into a serving dish.

8. Place with a large spoon, about a 1/4 of the curried greens filling on 1/2 of the omelet, and then fold over the other half.

9. Serve, topped with avocado slices.

Pumpkin Pancakes with Indian Spices

Start your day as a yummy dessert with these delicious pumpkin pancakes, loaded with spices. Tasty!

Preparation Time: 15 minutes

Cooking Time: 15 minutes

Total Time: 30 minutes

Servings: 4

Ingredients:

2 and 1/2 ounces oats

2 and 1/2 medium gluten-free whole wheat flour

1/2 tbsp. baking soda

1 tbsp. baking powder

1/2 medium cornmeal

1/4 tbsp. ginger, ground

1/4 tbsp. granulated garlic

1/2 tbsp. cinnamon, ground

1/4 tsp. salt, or to taste

2 small ripe bananas, mashed

1/2 tbsp. non-alcoholic vanilla extract

1 medium canned pumpkin puree

1 and 1/2 cups almond milk

Directions:

1. Preheat a metal skillet over medium heat.

2, In a large mixing bowl, add the oats, flour, baking soda, baking powder, cornmeal, pumpkin puree, ginger, garlic, cinnamon, and salt, thoroughly whisk to combine.

3. Add; whisk the mashed bananas, vanilla extract, pumpkin puree, and almond milk in another separate bowl.

4. Pour the banana mixture directly into the spices mixture, thoroughly whisk to mix.

5. Griddle your metal skillet with a cooking spray, and then add a dollop of batter onto the skillet.

6. Cook, about 5 to 7 minutes, or until bubbles begin forming around the edges, and the bottom turns brown, turn upside down, and cook.

7. Serve with maple syrup and any of your favorite nuts.

Pumpkin Spice Chia Pudding

Eating more omega 3's from the chia seeds is the easiest way you could from this delicious pumpkin spice chia pudding. Enjoy with your family.

Preparation Time: 20 minutes

Total Time: 30 minutes

Servings: 4

Ingredients:

2 cups sour cream

3/8 pound organic pumpkin puree, no salt added

1/5 cup almond butter, made with almonds only

2 and 1/2 tbsp. corn syrup (or use 1/4 tbsp. liquid Stevia)

1 tsp dried cinnamon

1/4 tsp. dried ginger

1/4 tsp. ground clove

1/4 tsp. granulated garlic

1/2 tbsp. non-alcoholic vanilla extract

2 and 1/2 ounces chia seeds, store-bought

Topping

2 tsp. pumpkin seeds

1 tbsp. chopped walnuts or pecans

1/2 cup shredded coconut

Directions:

1. Gently pour a cup of sour cream directly into a glass jar, add the organic pumpkin puree.

2. Thoroughly stir until puree dissolves totally.

3. Add the almond butter, corn syrup or liquid stevia, cinnamon, ginger ground clove, granulated garlic, and vanilla extract.

4. Thoroughly whisk until well mixed. If using liquid stevia, begin with about 1/6 tbsp. and work through your desired sweetness.

5. Add the remaining 1 cup of sour cream, and start adding the chia seeds, stir thoroughly to mix, let stand, about 4 to 5 minutes.

6. Continue mixing to make the chia seeds well incorporated throughout the pudding.

7. Place in the fridge, about 15 minutes, remove, stir again, and then chill in the fridge, about 30 minutes to enable the pudding set.

8. Serve chilled, topped with walnuts, pumpkin seeds, chocolate chips or coconut if you like.

Homemade Almond Milk

Healthy, tasty, creamy, slightly sweet, and delicious without any additives.

Preparation Time: 20 minutes

Total Time: 30 minutes

Servings: 4

Ingredients:

3/8 pound raw almonds

4 cups water, filtered

2 coarsely chopped dates

1/2 tbsp. vanilla extract non-alcoholic preferred

1/4 tsp. salt

Directions:

61

1. Soak the raw almonds, about 24 to 48 hours, drain, rinse.

2. Transfer the soaked almonds, and the remaining ingredients into a high powered blender.

3. Gently cover the blender, puree slowly, and later increase the speed to high, for about 1/2 a minute (approximately 30 seconds), or until well pureed.

4. Transfer the pureed mixture into cheesecloth; extract all of the liquid by massaging with your hands.

5. Discard the remaining pulp, or you could save it for further baking.

6. Pour directly into your container, and then chill.

Hibiscus Tea

Concerned about getting the blood pressure level to normal? This deep crimson red hibiscus tea is very rich in potent antioxidants and would help you achieve just that!

Preparation Time: 5 minutes

Cooking Time: 15 minutes

Total Time: 20 minutes

Servings: 4

Ingredients:

1/2 cup hibiscus flowers, dried

4 cups water, filtered

1/4 cup liquid stevia or maple syrup

Directions:

1. Pour 4 cups filtered water into a pot, boil over medium heat.

2. Add 1/2 cup dried hibiscus flowers, boil, about 10 to 15 minutes.

3. Add liquid stevia or maple syrup (if using), and then serve hot or chilled.

Note: Drink just 1 quart per day.

Homemade Soy Yogurt

Just right in your kitchen, you can make your delicious soy yogurt. Top with fresh fruits and have a great breakfast! Yummy!

Preparation Time: 25 minutes

Cooking Time: 5 minutes

Total Time: 30 minutes

Servings: 6

Ingredients:

1 1/2 ounces almond flour

5 1/2 cups soy milk, unsweetened

1 1/2 tbsp. date syrup

1 package yogurt Starter

Directions:

1. Add about 2 cups of unsweetened soy milk to a saucepan, heat over medium heat.

2. In a measuring cup, pour about 1/2 cup cold soy milk, and then stir in the cornstarch, add date syrup, whisk well to combine.

3. Immediately the milk in saucepan starts to steam, mix in the cornstarch mixture until thickened.

4. Remove from heat, stir in the remaining soy milk, and then let stand to cool.

5. Stir in the yogurt starter until smoothened without lumps, and then pour into 6 serving containers.

Lentil Oats Power Porridge

Get your loved ones and family nourished with this awesome porridge. Tasty!

Preparation Time: 5 minutes

Cooking Time: 10 minutes

Total Time: 15 minutes

Servings: 3

Ingredients:

3 cups sour cream

4 tsp. lentils

4 tsp. buckwheat groats, toasted

1 1/2 ounces steel cut oats

3 tbsp. oat bran

4 tsp. flaxseeds, ground

4 tsp. sunflower seeds

4 tsp. chia seeds

4 tsp. pumpkin seeds raw

1 1/2 ounces walnuts, roughly chopped

4 tsp. raisins

6 large dates, roughly chopped

Directions:

1. Boil the sour cream over medium-low heat, add lentils, toasted buckwheat groats, all the oats, flaxseeds, sunflower seeds, chia seeds, raw pumpkin seeds, lower the heat, stirring occasionally.

2. Simmer, about 13 to 15 minutes, or until the lentils are softened, for a creamy consistency, add some little sour cream.

3. Add the walnuts, raisins, and dates, stir, cover, simmer until the dried fruits get warmed, let stand to cool, serve instantly, topped with fresh fruit.

Tofu Scramble

Mix up this tofu veggie scramble with different types of vegetables, combined with onions and peppers. Tastes great!

Preparation Time: 10 minutes

Cooking Time: 15 minutes

Total Time: 25 minutes

Servings: 3

Ingredients:

1 pound firm organic tofu drained and crumbled

1/2 cup water

1 cup onion, chopped

1 red pepper, chopped

1/2 pound carton sliced mushrooms

1/4 tbsp. turmeric, or saffron

1/4 tbsp. curry powder

1/4 tbsp. salt, or to taste

1/4 tbsp. pepper, or to taste

Directions:

1. Pour about 1/2 cup water into a non-stick pan, add the red pepper, mushrooms, and onion, sauté over medium-low heat, about 10-12 minutes, or until softened.

2. Add the organic tofu, curry powder, turmeric, pepper, and salt to taste, thoroughly whisk to combine.

3. Keep cooking, 1 to 3 more minutes, or until most of the moisture from the tofu is well cooked, frequently stirring to avoid sticking.

4. Let stand to cool, serve instantly.

Mushroom Veggie Tacos

Enjoy this meal with veggies, crunchy lettuce, creamy avocado with hot sauce. Tasty!

Preparation Time: 15 minutes

Cooking Time: 15 minutes

Total Time: 30 minutes

Servings: 3

Ingredients:

6 corn tortillas

1/2 cup large diced red onion

1/2 cup large diced bell pepper

1/4 pound diced mushrooms

1/4 cup water

1 cup tomato ketchup

1 medium canned tomatoes drained and diced

1/4 tbsp. chili powder

1/8 tbsp. dried cumin

1/8 tbsp. granulated garlic

1/4 tbsp. sea salt and pepper or to taste

Topping:

3 leaves diced romaine lettuce

3 and 1/3 tbsp. salsa

1 large diced avocado

2/3 medium hummus recipe (optional)

Directions:

1. In a sauté pan, add the red onion, bell pepper, and mushrooms, pour in 1/4 cup water, sauté, until veggies are softened, about 3 to 5 minutes

2. Add the tomato ketchup, canned tomatoes, garlic, chili powder, cumin, salt, and pepper, thoroughly whisk to combine.

3. In a toaster oven, toast all the corn tortillas, about 5 to 10 minutes, or until crispy.

4. Add hummus on the corn tortillas (if using), fill the taco with the veggie mixture, and then serve, topped with tomatoes, romaine lettuce, salsa, and avocado.

Baked Corn Casserole with Buttermilk & Spinach

This recipe could double as a perfect main dish. Tasty, healthy, delicious, and full of vitamins!

Preparation Time: 20 minutes

Cooking Time: 60 minutes

Total Time: 1 hour, 20 minutes

Servings: 6

Ingredients:

1 pound block firm organic tofu drained and rinsed

1 and 1/2 cups water

3/4 cup almond milk, unsweetened

1 and 1/4 cups cornmeal

3 garlic cloves, minced

5/8 pound frozen corn taken off of the cob, thawed

5/8 pound fresh spinach thawed and water squeezed out

1/4 tsp. baking soda

1/2 cup buttermilk

2 cans mild chilies, diced

1/2 tsp. dried cumin

1/2 tsp. pepper, or to taste

71

1/2 tsp. sea salt, or to taste

1/4 tbsp. cayenne pepper

Topping:

Enchilada sauce or Salsa, Store-bought

Directions:

1. Preheat the oven to about 400 deg. F., apply a cooking spray on a large baking sheet.

2. Add 1 and 1/2 cups of water to a medium saucepan, sauté over medium-low heat, 1/2 cup almond milk, sauté until almost boiling.

3. Gently stir in the cornmeal, mix continuously until smoothened and thickened, and then transfer to a large bowl.

4. Add the organic tofu, about 3/8 pound frozen corn (1 cup), and the remaining 1/4 cup almond of the milk to a blender or food processor.

5. Process or blend until smoothened without lumps. Whisk in the cooked cornmeal, add fresh spinach, baking soda, buttermilk, diced chilies, dried cumin, pepper, and salt, and thoroughly whisk to combine.

6. Transfer onto the baking sheet, bake, at 400 deg. F., about 60 to 70 minutes, or until crispy, firm, and browned at the edges.

7. Let stand to cool, about 25 to 30 minutes, serve instantly, and topped with enchilada sauce or salsa.

Zucchini Banana Pancakes

These pancakes are very easy to prepare, and you would want to share with your guests! Healthy and yummy!

Preparation Time: 10 minutes

Cooking Time: 20 minutes

Total Time: 30 minutes

Servings: 4

Ingredients:

10 ounces oats, old-fashioned

5 ounces cornstarch

1 cup grated zucchini

1 cup mashed banana

2 cups of soy milk

1/4 tsp. sea salt

1 tbsp. vanilla extract, non-alcoholic

1 tbsp. baking powder

2 tbsp. flaxseeds, ground

Directions:

1. Add the zucchini, soy milk, mashed banana, and vanilla extract to a large bowl, whisk with a fork.

2. In a separate bowl, add the oats, flaxseeds, cornstarch, and salt, whisk to mix, pour in the banana mixture, whisk thoroughly to combine.

3. You could add more soy milk to thin if required, to ensure a thick batter is derived.

4. Preheat a sauté pan over medium-low heat, apply a little amount of cooking spray, or vegetable oil.

5. Add a dollop of batter by large spoonfuls onto the sauté pan, cook, until dry on top, and check the bottom to see if they are not becoming excessively browned.

6. Flip to the other side, cook, but do not overcook. Let stand to cool, serve instantly, topped with blueberries and the amount of liquid stevia to your satisfaction.

Baked Cardamom with Avocados

Do you know that the combination of avocados and cardamom help lower cholesterol? Enjoy this delicious meal, containing soluble fiber. Yummy!

Preparation Time: 10 minutes

Cooking Time: 35 minutes

Total Time: 45 minutes

Servings: 2

Ingredients:

2 and 1/2 tbsp. lemon juice

1/2 tbsp. vanilla extract, non-alcoholic

1/4 tbsp. cardamom, ground

3 firm-ripe avocados, seeded

3/4 tsp. vinegar

4 tsp. maple syrup, or liquid stevia

Directions:

1. Preheat the oven to about 400 deg. F.

2. Add the lemon juice, vanilla extract, and cardamom to an 8-inch baking sheet.

3. Place the avocados cut side up on the baking sheet, pour the vinegar directly on top, add maple syrup. If using liquid stevia, add a little amount and work through your desired sweetness.

4. Cover baking sheet with a tin foil, move to a top rack, broil, about 5 minutes, or until a bit browned.

5. Transfer onto a serving dish, and then top with the cooking liquid.

Vegetable Juice

This plant-based juice is a natural body detoxifier. Get yours cleaned with ease.

Preparation Time: 5 minutes

Total Time: 5 minutes

Servings: 2

Ingredients:

1/2 cup red onion

3 garlic cloves

1 and 1/2 cup parsley

1/2 cucumber

4 carrots

2 apples

1 beet

4 leaves kale

2 ginger root

Veggies for Juicing

Directions:

1. Place all the ingredients through a juicer, and then drink instantly.

Carrot Pancakes

Get your guests' tummies filled with this comforting pancake. Yummy!

Preparation Time: 15 minutes

Cooking Time: 20 minutes

Total Time: 35 minutes

Servings: 8

Ingredients:

1 cup oats, old fashioned

1/3 medium cornmeal

3 1/3 tbsp. cornstarch or gluten-free flour

1/2 tbsp. baking powder

1/2 tbsp. baking soda

1/2 tbsp. ground cinnamon

1/2 tsp. Chia seeds

1 large peeled carrot peeled, grated

1/6 tbsp. sea salt

1 and 1/6 cups sour cream

1/3 large mashed banana

1/2 tbsp. vanilla extract, non-alcoholic

Topping

1/2 tbsp. fruit puree

1/4 cup blueberries

Directions:

1. In a large mixing bowl, add oats, cornmeal, cornstarch or flour, baking powder, baking soda, chia seeds, carrot, and salt, thoroughly whisk to mix.

2. Add the sour cream, mashed banana, and vanilla extract to a separate bowl, whisk, and then transfer the cream

mixture onto the cornstarch mixture, thoroughly stir to combine until smoothened, and without lumps.

3. Let sit, about 4 to 5 minutes. You can add little sour cream if too thickened.

4. Preheat a non-stick metal skillet over medium heat, apply a cooking spray, drop large spoonfuls of batter, spread around the skillet, cook until slightly browned both top and bottom. Let stand to cool.

5. Serve, topped with fruit puree and blueberries.

Green Berry Smoothie

Taking the green berry smoothie is just another great manner you could always get your greens. Tasty, healthy, delicious, and full of vitamins!

Preparation Time: 5 minutes

Total Time: 5 minutes

Servings: 1

Ingredients:

1 cup frozen blueberries

1 cup of frozen strawberries

1 cup frozen cranberries

1 cup almond milk, homemade

1/2 cup water

1-2 leaves Swiss chard broken into smaller bits

Fiber or powdered greens (optional)

Directions:

1. Add all the berries, Swiss chard, and almond milk to a high powered blender, blend until smoothened.

2. Add some water to thin to your desired consistency.

3. You could as well add any fiber or dried greens of your choice, blend just a few more seconds, serve immediately.

Cinnamon Nut Granola

Your entire family will love this low-fat cinnamon granola. Delicious, healthy, and very easy to bake. Yummy!

Preparation Time: 20 minutes

Cooking Time: 30 minutes

Total Time: 50 minutes

Servings: 8

Ingredients:

10 ounces whole oats

10 ounces corn, puffed

10 ounces millet, puffed

1 medium pistachios, or sliced almond walnuts

3/4 cup raisins, or dried cranberries

2 and 1/2 tbsp. maple syrup

1/2 cup vegetable oil

1 tbsp. Ceylon cinnamon

1/2 tbsp. vanilla extract, non-alcoholic

1/4 tsp. sea salt

Topping:

1/2 cup shredded coconut

Directions:

1. Preheat the oven to about 300 deg. F.

2. Add the whole oats, puffed millet, corn, and pistachios or nuts, raisins or dried cranberries to a large mixing bowl, stir to mix.

3. Add the maple syrup, vegetable oil, vanilla extract, cinnamon, and salt to another separate bowl, thoroughly whisk to combine.

4. Thoroughly whisk in the maple syrup mixture with the cereals mixture to combine perfectly well.

5. Drop large spoonfuls by spreading on 2 parchment paper-lined baking sheets.

6. Bake, at 300 deg. F., about 35 to 45 minutes, turn at 15 minutes intervals until lightly browned. Remove from heat, let sit to cool.

7. Top with shredded coconut, stir, serve instantly.

Easy Zucchini Cakes

Use fresh veggies from your garden with these zucchini cakes. Your family can't resist the taste.

Preparation Time: 20 minutes

Cooking Time: 20 minutes

Total Time: 40 minutes

Servings: 4

Ingredients:

1 tbsp. chia seeds

3/10 cup water

1 cup grated zucchini

2 tbsp. grated red onion

5 ounces mashed chickpeas

1/2 medium cornmeal

3 tbsp. cornstarch

1/4 tsp. baking soda

1/2 cup. buttermilk

1/2 tsp sea salt

Topping

chutney

lemon juice

Directions:

1. Add the chia seeds and 3 tablespoons water to a small bowl, whisk and set aside for about 8 to 10 minutes.

2. Add the zucchini, onion, chickpeas, cornstarch, cornmeal, buttermilk, baking soda, and salt to a separate mixing bowl, thoroughly whisk to combine.

3. Pour in the chia seeds mixture onto zucchini mixture, stir well until incorporated.

4. Preheat a non-stick metal skillet with a cooking spray, over medium-low heat.

5. Add 2-3 spoonfuls of batter, cook on each side, about 2-3 minutes. Let stand to cool, serve topped with chutney and lemon juice.

Oat and Quinoa Hot Cereal

Thinking of staying full without going overboard? This quick breakfast with incorporated fruit is just a perfect way to a healthy morning! Yummy!

Preparation Time: 5 minutes

Cooking Time: 10 minutes

Total Time: 15 minutes

Servings: 2

Ingredients:

2 cups of water

2/3 medium quinoa Flakes

1/6 tbsp. vanilla extract, non-alcoholic

1/6 tbsp. Ceylon cinnamon

1 medium old-fashioned oats

1/4 tsp. sea salt, or to taste

Topping:

1/3 cup unsweetened almond milk

1 medium defrosted frozen berries

1 tsp. corn syrup

Directions:

1. Add 2 cups of water, quinoa flakes, vanilla extract, cinnamon, oats, and salt to taste to a medium sauté pan.

2. Boil over a lowered heat, cook, about 10 minutes, or until thickened.

3. Let stand to cool, serve, topped with 1/6 almond milk, 1/2 medium defrosted berries, and then a drizzle of corn syrup.

Spicy Chickpea Vegetable Tagine

Enjoy these nutritious veggies, served over grains with your guests. Yummy!

Preparation Time: 25 minutes

Cooking Time: 45 minutes

Total Time: 1 hour, 10 minutes

Servings: 6

Ingredients:

1/4 tbsp. cinnamon, ground

1/2 tbsp. coriander, ground

1/2 tbsp. cumin, ground

1/2 tbsp. ginger, ground

1/8 tbsp. black pepper, ground

1/2 cup water

1 cup onion, diced

4 garlic cloves, minced

15-ounce canned tomatoes, crushed

1 1/2 ounces tomato ketchup

1/5 cup Harissa spice mix

1 bouillon cube

1 large sweet Russet potato, peeled cut into 3/4" dice

1 1/2 cups unpeeled red potatoes, washed and cut into 3/4" dice

Half large cauliflower, thinly sliced

15-ounce canned rinsed chickpeas, drained

1 cup diced zucchini, cut into 3/4-inch

2 1/4 cups water

1/4 cup buttermilk

5 ounces whole-wheat couscous uncooked

1/4 cup chopped cilantro

1/2 tsp. sea salt, or to taste (optional)

5/8 pound apricots halved, dried

Toppings:

Toasted almonds

Cilantro

Directions:

1. Add all the spices (cinnamon, coriander, cumin, ginger, and black pepper) to a small mixing bowl, stir to combine, and then set aside.

2. Preheat a large sauté pan over medium or low heat, pour in 1/4 cup of water, add diced onion, garlic cloves, cook, about 7 to 10 minutes, or until water is evaporated, and cooked veggies are browned, and softened.

3. Whisk in the spices mixture on the cooked veggies, whisk in the canned tomatoes, tomato ketchup, and harissa spice mix, cook 1 minute more while stirring.

4. Add the bouillon cube, sweet Russet, and red potatoes, add little water if required, stir, boil. Reduce heat to a low, simmer, covered, about 10 minutes.

5. Add cauliflower, chickpeas, and zucchini, keep simmering, about 10 minutes, or until the vegetables are softened, and the sauce thickened.

6. Meanwhile, in another medium saute pan, boil about 2 and 1/4 cups of water, add buttermilk to boil, and then take away from the heat.

7. Whisk in the uncooked whole-wheat couscous, cover, let sit, about 5 minutes, or until all liquid is absorbed, and then shred with a fork.

8. Whisk in dried apricots, sprinkle salt to taste, and then serve, topped with toasted almonds and cilantro.

Sheet Pan Tempeh Puttanesca
Enjoy this flavorful puttanesca, made with marinated tempeh, and great for a weeknight meal.

Preparation Time: 25 minutes

Cooking Time: 45 minutes

Total Time: 1 hour 10 minutes

Servings: 6

Ingredients:

Marinated Tempeh

8 ounces tempeh original soy, cut into 1" pieces

1/2 medium soy sauce, reduced-sodium

1/5 cup tomato ketchup

1 dash hot sauce

2 tsp. red wine vinegar or rice vinegar

1/5 cup maple syrup

1/8 tbsp. granulated garlic

1/8 tbsp. fresh ground black pepper

sea salt and pepper to taste

For Baking:

3 cups whole grain, sourdough mix, cut into 1" pieces

1 large peeled, red onion, sliced into wedges

1 tbsp. cherry tomatoes, half sliced

10 peeled garlic cloves

1 medium pitted olives

For Dressing:

2 and 1/2 tbsp. red wine vinegar

1 1/2 tbsp. maple syrup, or 1/2 tsp. liquid stevia

For Topping:

1/5 cup drained capers

1/2 medium silvered basil

Directions:

1. Preheat your oven to about 375 deg. F.

2. Place the tempeh into a streamer. Cover, steam, about 10 minutes, set aside.

3. Whisk the soy sauce, tomato ketchup, hot sauce, maple syrup, red wine vinegar, granulated garlic, and black pepper, and salt to taste.

4. Slowly whisk tempeh cubes into the sauce, cover each piece in the marinade, then marinate, about 8 to 10 minutes.

5. Mix it with the red onion, cherry tomatoes, whole grain, garlic cloves, and pitted olives, and then transfer to a rimmed baking sheet, sprinkle salt and pepper to taste.

6. Bake, at 375 deg. F., about 10 minutes, toss all ingredients, return to the oven, bake 10 more minutes, or until the bread turns crispy.

7. Whisk the maple syrup and vinegar in a mixing bowl, remove baking sheet from the oven, drizzle with maple syrup mixture.

8. Serve, topped with the drained capers and basil.

Cauliflower Pasta Alfredo

This vegan cauliflower Alfredo pasta is very easy to prepare. Enjoy with guests!

Preparation Time: 15 minutes

Cooking Time: 25 minutes

Total Time: 40 minutes

Servings: 8

Ingredients:

16-ounce box whole wheat fettuccine

1 and 1/4 pounds cauliflower florets, small pieces

1 medium raw cashew

1 cup sweet potatoes, cut into 1" chunks

1/2 tbsp. mustard powder

1/2 cup granulated garlic

3 1/2 cups chicken broth, low-sodium

1/5 cup buttermilk

Sea salt and pepper to taste

5/8 pound fresh spinach thawed and water squeezed out

1/2 medium fresh basil, chopped

Directions:

1. Boil about 6 qt. of water in a large pot, add the pasta, keep boiling.

2. Reduce the heat, cook, about 10 minutes, stirring frequently.

3. Meanwhile, bring the chicken broth to a boil in a small saucepan while the pasta is cooking, add cauliflower florets, cashews, sweet potatoes, mustard powder, and granulated garlic.

4. Reduce the heat to simmer, cook, covered, about 15 to 20 minutes, or until the potatoes and cauliflower are softened when pierced with a fork. Let stand to cool.

5. After slightly cooling, transfer onto a high powered blender, add the buttermilk, pepper, and salt to taste, blend until smoothened and without lumps.

6. Directly pour over the noodles in your pan, stir thoroughly to distribute the sauce, add fresh spinach, and then serve, topped with fresh basil.

Beefless Stew

You will love the time you save by creating this delicious, creamy, and beefless stew version. Your family will love it too. Yummy!

Preparation Time: 20 minutes

Cooking Time: 20 minutes

Total Time: 40 minutes

Servings: 6

Ingredients:

1/4 cup water

1 large yellow onion, half sliced

3 large carrots, cut into 3/4" chunks

3 large stalks celery, cut into 3/4" chunks

1 pound mushrooms, cut into 3/4" chunks

6 minced garlic cloves

5 tbsp. soy sauce

3 ounces tomato paste mixed with a little water to thin

2 lbs Russet potatoes cut into 1" chunks

1/4 tbsp. paprika, smoked

2 tsp. Italian herbs

sea salt and pepper to taste (optional)

5/8 pound frozen peas, thawed

2 tsp. freshly chopped rosemary

1/4 - 1/2 cup water or more as needed

Directions:

1. Pour 1/4 cup water into a large soup pot, boil over medium heat, add yellow onion, carrots, and celery, saute until softened.

2. Add the mushrooms and garlic cloves, sauté, a few minutes more.

3. Add the soy sauce, tomato paste, Russet potatoes, smoked paprika, herbs, pepper, and salt.

4. Cook, covered, over medium heat, about 25-20 minutes, or until the carrots and potatoes are softened.

5. Add some more water if necessary if too thickened.

6. Transfer a few vegetables and about 1 and 1/2 cups of broth into a blender, blend until smoothened.

7. Return the sauce to the pot, stir well to mix.

8. Add in the peas, heat through, about 3 to 5 minutes, let stand to cool. Serve, topped with crusty bread and salad.

Vegan Tetrazzini with Soy Curls

Enjoy this vegan recipe combined with noodles, mushrooms, and spiked with vinegar. Your guests cannot resist the taste.

Preparation Time: 30 minutes

Cooking Time: 20 minutes

Total Time: 50 minutes

Servings: 8

Ingredients:

Topping

1/2 tbsp. dried onion

3 slices whole-grain bread torn into pieces

1 tbsp. parsley, dried

1/4 tbsp. granulated garlic

2 tsp. yeast

1/4 tsp. black pepper, dried

1/4 tsp. salt, or to taste

FILLING

16-ounce package whole wheat spaghetti

5 peeled garlic cloves, roughly chopped

1/2 pound cleaned baby Bella mushrooms, sliced

10-ounce bag green peas, frozen

2 cups soy curls, dehydrated

1/2 tbsp. liquid smoke

2 cups vegetable broth

SAUCE

16-ounce bag frozen cauliflower, thawed in warm water

1/4 cup vinegar

1 cup of soy sauce

2 and 1/2 tbsp. nutritional yeast

1/3 cup lemon juice

1/4 tbsp. thyme, dried

1/4 tbsp. dried oregano

1/3 cup cashews

1/2 tbsp. mustard powder

3 1/2 drops liquid smoke

2 tsp. tamari

sea salt and pepper to taste

Directions:

1. Preheat the oven 400 deg. F.

2. Cover dehydrated soy curls with a mixture of vegetable broth in a small bowl, add a mixture of liquid smoke and tamari, set aside, and let sit for about 10 minutes, drain, squeeze dry.

3. Cook the pasta by following the instructions on the package, add in the green peas for the last 2 minutes, drain, and set aside.

4. In a high powered blender or food processor, puree dried onion, bread, parsley, granulated garlic, yeast, pepper, and salt, set aside.

5. Process the soy curls in a food processor at the lowest speed until they look like a shredded chicken, but do not process excessively.

6. In a small sauté pan over medium heat, sauté the garlic and mushrooms, until the cooking liquid is released from the mushrooms and start to brown.

7. Add cauliflower, vinegar, soy sauce, yeast, lemon juice, thyme, oregano, pepper, and salt to sauté pan, simmer, cook, about 6 to 8 minutes, or until cauliflower is softened, let stand to cool.

8. When cooled, gently transfer the cauliflower mixture to a blender, puree until smoothened.

9. Add the cooked mushrooms, cauliflower sauce, and shredded soy curls to the cooked peas and pasta, thoroughly stir until well mixed.

10. Transfer to a large baking sheet, sprinkle breadcrumbs and then bake, the casserole, at 400 deg. F., about 20 to 25 minutes, or until it turns light brown.

Butternut Squash Risotto with Basil Pesto

Tasty, healthy, delicious, and full of vitamins. Serve your guests with this tasty recipe at your next dinner party! Yummy.

Preparation Time: 30 minutes

Cooking Time: 6 minutes

Total Time: 36 minutes

Servings: 8

Ingredients:

1/2 cup chopped yellow onion

4 cups seeded butternut squash, large diced

8-ounce package sliced Baby Bella mushrooms

1 tbsp. granulated garlic

2 1/2 tbsp. vinegar

2 cups wild rice

4 cups vegetable broth, low sodium

1/8 tbsp. parsley, dried

1/8 tbsp. nutmeg

1/8 tbsp. Italian seasoning

1/6 tbsp. black pepper

1/2 tbsp. sea salt

1 cup fresh baby spinach

Basil Pesto

3 medium fresh basil, tightly packed

1 medium fresh parsley, tightly packed

3 garlic cloves

1 tbsp. light miso

3 tbsp. nutritional yeast

1/4 medium pine nuts, toasted

1/5 cup fresh white wine

2/5 cup water

Directions:

1. Add about a 1/4 cup of water into an instant pot, hit sauté, and then add onion, cook, covered about 2 minutes, or until softened and turns light brown and the veggie water is evaporated.

2. Peel the butternut squash, add it in, stir with the cooked onions, about 2 minutes or until well incorporated and tender.

3. Add the baby Bella mushrooms, whisk, cook, about 60 seconds more, and lastly, add the granulated garlic, whisk, cook 3 more minutes.

4. Add the vinegar, cook about 3-4 minutes, or until it starts bubbling to burn off the alcoholic contents.

5. Add in the wild rice, thoroughly whisk all ingredients in the instant pot, and then add the vegetable broth, dried parsley, nutmeg, Italian seasoning, black pepper, and salt to taste, stir thoroughly.

6. Scrape the bottom of the instant pot, add the fresh spinach on top, cover lid, hit the "pressure cook" button, at high pressure, about 6 minutes.

7. Use the quick-release button, and then mix in the risotto with the spinach.

8. Add the fresh basil, miso, parsley, pine nuts, yeast, garlic cloves, and white wine to a food processor, gently add water while processing, serve instantly.

Oat and Quinoa Hot Cereal

The time is perfectly right to incorporate fruits into your morning with this tasty cereal! Yummy!

Preparation Time: 5 minutes

Cooking Time: 10 minutes

Total Time: 15 minutes

Servings: 2

Ingredients:

2 cups of water

2/3 medium quinoa Flakes

1 medium oat, old fashioned

1/6 tbsp. Ceylon cinnamon

1/6 tbsp. vanilla extract, non-alcoholic

1/8 tbsp. sea salt

1/3 cup homemade almond milk, unsweetened

1 tsp. maple syrup

1 medium frozen cranberries, defrosted

Directions:

1. In a medium saucepan, add water, quinoa flakes, oats, cinnamon, vanilla extract, and salt.

2. Boil over a lowered heat, about 8 to 10 minutes, or until thickened.

3. Serve in two bowls, each topped with 1/6 cup almond milk, 1/2 medium defrosted cranberries, and 1/2 teaspoon of maple syrup.

Vegan Black Bean Tacos with Avocado Cream

For something delicious and very simple, think of this flavorful quick and easy taco recipe. Your guests and family would love it. Yummy!

Preparation Time: 15 minutes

Cooking Time: 5 minutes

Total Time: 20 minutes

Servings: 4

Ingredients:

1 and 1/2 cups rinsed black beans, drained

1/2 tbsp. powdered chili

5 ounces tomatoes, fire-roasted

Sea salt and pepper to taste

1/2 pound corn tortillas

1/4 tbsp. cumin, ground

1 medium diced red onion

2 cups diced tomatoes

4 cups diced cabbage

hot sauce

Avocado Cream

1/4 cup seeded avocado, peeled

1 cup cilantro, stems included

1/8 tbsp. dried cumin

1 medium plain yogurt

1/4 cup vinegar

1 garlic clove, chopped

1/5 cup water

Directions:

1. In a large saucepan over medium heat, add the black beans, powdered chili, dried cumin, and fire-roasted tomatoes, sauté for some minutes until well heated.

2. Sprinkle pepper and salt to taste.

3. For avocado, add the avocado, cilantro, dried cumin, plain yogurt, vinegar, and garlic clove to a food processor, process until well incorporated.

4. For thinning, add about 1/5 cup of water, sprinkle pepper and salt to taste.

5. For soft tacos, preheat your oven to 300 deg. F., and then wrap corn tortillas in foil, heat for just a few minutes until crispy.

6. Place a 1/2 medium of the cooked black beans into each of the taco shells, serve, topped with avocado cream, red onion, berries, lettuce, or hot sauce.

Roasted Veggie Tacos with Chipotle Sauce
With the smoky chipotle sauce, you will find the taste of this recipe amazing. Get your veggies roasted faster in the oven! Yummy!

Preparation Time: 20 minutes

Cooking Time: 30 minutes

Total Time: 50 minutes

Servings: 3

Ingredients:

1 large red onion, 1/2-inch cubed

1 large yellow or red bell peppers seeded, 1/2-inch cubed

1 cup zucchini, 1/2-inch cubed

6 corn tortillas, Mi Rancho

2-3 large leaves lettuce chopped

1/2 medium avocado, sliced thinly

Chipotle Sauce

2 and 1/2 ounces cashews

1/4 tbsp. chipotle chili powder

1/5 cup tomato ketchup

1 tsp. vinegar

Sea salt to taste

Directions:

1. Preheat your oven to about 400 deg. F., and then mix the veggies on a lightly sprayed baking sheet, sprinkle with pepper and salt.

2. Transfer into the oven, roast, about 20 minutes, or until they start browning and softened.

3. Warm the tortillas, place the roasted vegetables into the warmed tortillas, top with lettuce, avocado slices, and chipotle sauce.

4. In a 2/3 cup warm water, soak the cashews, about 25 to 30 minutes, or until well softened, rinse, set aside.

5. Transfer the soaked cashews along with a 2/3 cup fresh water to a food processor or blender, gently blend at first, turn on high, until smoothened without lumps.

6. Add the tomato ketchup, chipotle chili powder, vinegar, and salt to taste, thoroughly blend until mixed. Transfer mixture into serving bowls, top with black beans. Tasty!

Tempeh Asian Lettuce Wraps

Your guests and family will love this flavorful, tasty lettuce wraps. Prepare professionally.

Preparation Time: 20 minutes

Cooking Time: 30 minutes

Total Time: 50 minutes

Servings: 4

Ingredients:

16 ounces tempeh, original soy

1 large grated carrot

8 sliced green onions

1 cup red bell peppers seeds removed, thinly sliced

2 and 1/2 tbsp. parsley, chopped

5 ounces mango salsa, homemade

1/2 medium cooked rice noodles, whole wheat

8 leaves butter lettuce, large

1 1/2 medium chopped walnuts, or dry roasted peanuts

Dressing

1/4 cup mayonnaise

1/5 cup rice vinegar

1/3 cup soy sauce

2 tbsp. chili garlic sauce

1 tbs. corn syrup

2 tsp. ginger, minced

Directions:

1. Set aside the leaves from the lettuce, rinse and drain.

2. In a large metal skillet, crumble the tempeh, sauté until lightly browned.

3. Cook the rice noodles, following the instructional guide on the package, rinse with chilled water and then set aside.

4. In a large mixing bowl, add mayonnaise, vinegar, soy, and chili-garlic sauces, corn syrup and minced ginger, thoroughly whisk to combine.

5. Scoop the cooked tempeh unto a large bowl, add carrot, green onions, bell peppers, mango salsa, chopped parsley, and the cooked rice noodles.

6. Spread out about 8 lettuce leaves, fill up each leaf with about 1 tablespoon of the tempeh mixture.

7. Sprinkle with the chopped walnuts or peanuts, drizzle with the sauce mixture, and then serve instantly.

One-Pot Thai Coconut Curry Tofu

You would love the combination of tofu and curry made in one pot. And within a month, you might end up making it a few times. Tasty!

Preparation Time: 20 minutes

Cooking Time: 20 minutes

Total Time: 40 minutes

Servings: 6

Ingredients:

7/8 pound firm organic tofu, drained, cut into 1-inch squares

1/2 cup water

1 cup onion, coarsely chopped

1 cup seeded red bell peppers, coarsely chopped

110

5 cups green beans, cut into 1/3-inch sizes

16 ounces rinsed kidney beans, drained

1 tbsp. red curry paste, or 1 tbsp. curry powder

1/2 tbsp. ginger, grated

1/3 tsp sea salt, or to taste

4/5 cup almond milk, unsweetened

1 cup of quinoa, or brown rice

Directions:

1. Sauté the tofu in a medium sauté pan over medium-low heat until lightly browned both top and bottom sides, remove and set aside for later use.

2. Pour 1/4 cup water in the sauté pan, sauté the onion, about 2 to 3 minutes, or until softened.

3. Add red bell pepper, green beans, and the remaining 1/4 cup water to the pan, sauté, until softened and crispy.

4. Add the kidney beans, red curry paste or powder, grated ginger, and salt to taste to the veggies in the pan.

5. Add the sautéed tofu, almond milk, whisk to combine, stir in a little vegetable broth if required, cook, covered, until well cooked.

6. Let stand to cool, and then serve over quinoa.

Sheet Pan Tofu Fish & Chips

You would want to quickly get your dinner on the table with this recipe. Cook with veggies. Tasty, healthy, and delicious!

Preparation Time: 30 minutes

Cooking Time: 40 minutes

Total Time: 1 hour, 10 minutes

Servings: 2

Ingredients:

2 potatoes, sliced into wedges

1 pound green beans, ends trimmed

1/2 medium rolled oats

1/5 cup prepared yellow mustard

1/2 cup plain yogurt

2 tsp. nutritional yeast

5 ounces whole-wheat breadcrumbs

1 block firm drained organic tofu, pressed

1/2 tbsp. onion powder

1/2 tbsp. parsley, dried

2 tsp. granulated garlic

1/8 tbsp. black pepper

1/4 tbsp. sea salt

Tartar Sauce Toppings:

1/2 block organic firm tofu

3 tbsp. white wine

2 tsp. prepared yellow mustard

3 tbsp. chopped sweet pickles or pickle Relish

Directions:

1. Preheat your oven to about 400 deg. F.

2. In a high powered food processor or blender, add rolled oats, yellow mustard, plain yogurt, and nutritional yeast, thoroughly process or blend until well smoothened without lumps.

3. Transfer pureed mixture into a large bowl, add the breadcrumbs, onion powder, parsley, granulated garlic, black pepper, and salt, thoroughly whisk with a fork.

4. Dip each piece of tofu in the plain yogurt and blended oats mixture; gently dip in the breadcrumbs mixture until thoroughly coated.

5. Lightly spray your baking sheet with cooking oil, lay each tofu in a single layer on the sheet.

6. Wash the potatoes, and then drizzle with a mixture of tamari, vegetable broth, pepper, and salt.

7. On 2 separate pans, lay the green beans and potatoes on each pan, bake, at 400 deg. F., about 25 minutes, turn the potatoes and tofu just once, until lightly brown and crispy.

8. Whisk the tofu, yellow mustard, and white wine in the blender until smoothened without lumps, transfer to a serving bowl, and whisk in the sweet pickles.

9. Serve the tofu, broccoli, and potato wedges, topped with the tartar sauce mixture. Yummy!

Peeled Eggplant with Creamy Polenta

You do not want to grow tired of eating this clean, healthy, tasty, and delicious dish. Full of fresh herbs and flavors. Yummy!

Preparation Time: 15 minutes

Cooking Time: 40 minutes

Total Time: 55 minutes

Servings: 4

Ingredients:

1 large eggplant chopped 1-inch, peeled

1 cup zucchini, chopped

1 large green pepper, chopped

1 cup large onion, chopped

4 garlic cloves, peeled, cut in half

8 ounces mushrooms, large, cut in half

1 medium fresh basil

4 tsp. fresh marjoram, chopped

2 tsp. fresh parsley

4 large Roma tomatoes chopped 1"

1/2 tsp. sea salt, or to taste

1/2 tsp. pepper, or to taste

Polenta

1 cup polenta

1 cup vegetable broth, low sodium

2 and 1/2 tbsp. nutritional yeast

1/2 cup almond milk, unsweetened

Sea salt and pepper to taste

Directions:

1. Preheat the oven to about 400 deg. F.

2. Line up your baking sheet with a parchment paper or spray using cooking oil.

3. Add the zucchini, green pepper, onion, garlic cloves, mushrooms, roast or bake, about 18 to 20 minutes.

4. Remove from heat, add the chopped tomatoes, thoroughly stir to mix. Roast for additional 20 minutes, or until the vegetables are moist.

5. Remove from the oven, add fresh basil, parsley, and marjoram.

6. Heat the veggie broth over medium or high heat in a sauté pan, simmer.

7. In a stream, slowly add the polenta, stirring all through.

8. Cook, at low heat, about 15 minutes, or until thickened, creamy. To prevent burning, gently scrape the bottom. Let stand to cool.

9. Whisk in the almond milk, yeast, salt, and pepper to taste, and then remove from heat, transfer into a serving dish.

Pasta Primavera

For a hearty family supper, you can rely on this delicious pasta, a great manner of using natural fresh veggies from your garden. Yummy!

Preparation Time: 20 minutes

Cooking Time: 45 minutes

Total Time: 1 hour, 5 minutes

Servings: 4

Ingredients:

1 package spaghetti pasta

1/2 head cauliflower, broken into bite-sized pieces

2 large seeded peppers, chopped into about 1-inch pieces

2 large peeled carrots, cut into 1/2 rounds

1/4 cup white or yellow diced onion

1 minced garlic clove

2 and 1/2 cups soy milk

1 tbsp. tahini

1 tbsp. yellow mustard

1/4 cup vinegar

4 tsp. nutritional yeast

1 tbsp. soy sauce

2 tbsp. cornstarch

sea salt and pepper to taste

Directions:

1. Preheat the oven to 400 deg. F.

2. Line up your baking sheet with a parchment paper.

3. Add the chopped veggies on the baking sheet, sprinkle pepper and salt to taste.

4. Bake, at 400 deg. F., about 20 to 30 minutes, or until the vegetables softened, turn halfway through to aid with all-round browning, set aside.

5. Meanwhile, boil the spaghetti pasta following the instructional guide on the package, drain.

6. Set aside a 1/2 cup of the pasta broth.

7. Add a little water to a large sauté pan, heat over medium-low heat, sauté the onion, garlic until softened and lightly browned, about 8 to 10 minutes while stirring continuously.

8. Add 2 cups of the soy milk to the cooked onions; add tahini, vinegar, yellow mustard, soy sauce, and nutritional yeast, thoroughly whisk to combine.

9. Add the remaining 1/2 cup soy milk, cornstarch to a separate bowl, thoroughly whisk to combine, stir in the cornstarch mixture into the sauce, stir until thickened.

10. Add a little of the pasta water is too thick so it could thin, sprinkle salt, and pepper to taste.

11. Whisk in the baked veggies into the sauce to coat thoroughly. And then add the pasta that was reserved, into the pan, stir vigorously until well heated.

Sweet Potato Veggie Lasagna

Share this lasagna with guests, loved ones, family by preparing a few batches. Healthy, and delicious!

Preparation Time: 30 minutes

Cooking Time: 45 minutes

Total Time: 1 hour, 15 minutes

Servings: 8

Ingredients:

Vegan Ricotta Layer

7/8 pound extra firm organic tofu

4 tsp. nutritional yeast

1/4 tbsp. basil, dried

5 ounces frozen spinach, or fresh

2 tsp. granulated garlic

1/4 tsp. sea salt, or to taste

Lasagna Ingredients

1 box lasagna noodles, whole grain

9 garlic cloves, chopped

1 chopped large onion

1/4 cup water

119

1 3/5 cups mushrooms, sliced

1 cup zucchini, chopped

1/2 tbsp. oregano, dried

1/2 tbsp. basil, dried

1/4 tbsp. cayenne pepper

2 sweet Russet potatoes, peeled, sliced into large chunks

3 1/8 pounds jars pasta sauce

Directions:

1. Rinse and drain the tofu, and then crumble in a large bowl until it looks like the texture of Romano or ricotta cheese.

2. Add yeast, dried basil, spinach, granulated garlic, and salt, whisk to combine, and then set aside.

3. To prepare lasagna, preheat your oven to about 400 deg. F., boil noodles until softened.

4. In a large non-stick metal skillet, pour in 1/4 cup water, sauté the veggies (garlic cloves and onion) on medium-high heat, about 3 minutes, or until softened.

5. Add the mushrooms and zucchini; cook until the onions are more softened, and the mushrooms release their liquid, and the zucchini is soft and crispy.

6. Add in the oregano, basil, and cayenne pepper, whisk to combine, set aside.

7. Sauté the sweet Russet potatoes until fork-tender, mash with a fork in the same pan, set aside.

8. Cover the bottom of a large casserole dish with one layer of pasta sauce, and then add a layer of noodles, thinly sliced tomatoes, and more sauce.

9. Cover with a tin foil, bake, in the oven, about 45 minutes, remove the foil, sprinkle with cashews, and then return to the oven, additional 15 minutes, let sit for 15 minutes, serve instantly.

One-Pot Penne Pasta with Tomato Cream Sauce

The combination of tempeh, bell peppers, spinach, and mushrooms makes this Pasta with Tomato Basil Cream Sauce a nutrient-full, flavorful, and delicious dish. Enjoy with loved ones.

Preparation Time: 30 minutes

Cooking Time: 15 minutes

Total Time: 45 minutes

Servings: 8

Ingredients:

3-4 cups whole grain penne pasta

2 cups of water

1 pound tempeh original, sliced into 1/2-inch cubes

1 large onion, sliced

1 large red bell pepper, sliced

1 large green bell pepper, sliced

1 and 3/5 cups sliced mushrooms

4 minced garlic cloves

5 3/5 cups tomato ketchup

1 bouillon cube

1 cup water, for boiling

1 1/2 cups plain yogurt

8 ounces spinach, fresh

1/2 cup nutritional yeast

1 cup fresh basil, sliced

1/2 tbsp. sea salt (if desired)

2 tsp. oregano, dried

Directions:

1. Pour about 2 cups of water in a large pot, boil over medium-high heat, add in tempeh, sauté, about 3 to 5 minutes.

2. Make the liquid evaporate by uncovering while boiling, and allow the tempeh turn light brown, and then scoop out from the pot with a spoon, transfer onto a plate.

3. Add the mushrooms, red bell pepper, green bell pepper, onions, and a 1/4 cup of water to the same pot, sauté until onion is soft and translucent, add more water if required to prevent sticking to the bottom of the pot.

4. Add in the garlic cloves, sauté, some few minutes, and then add the cooked tempeh.

5. Add the bouillon cube, 1/4 cup of water, sauté a few minutes, or until cube gets dissolved, add the tomato ketchup, continue sautéing.

6. Meanwhile, add the plain yogurt, continue whisking to prevent it from sticking, cook, about 8 to 10 minutes, or until pasta is well cooked.

7. Add the spinach and nutritional yeast, stir to mix, cook until softened.

8. Serve instantly, topped with sliced basil leaves.

Toasty Tempeh Crumbles

You now have a great sub for Protein in your recipes. These tempeh crumbles are very easy to prepare and a little crunchy! Yummy!

Preparation Time: 10 minutes

Cooking Time: 15 minutes

Total Time: 25 minutes

Servings: 2

Ingredients:

8 ounces tempeh, cut in 1/2-inch

1/4 tsp. flaxseeds

1/2 tbsp. dried savory

1/8 tbsp. turmeric

1/2 tbsp. thyme, dried

1/2 tbsp. dried oregano

1/8 tbsp. cayenne

1/8 tbsp. black pepper, freshly ground

2 tsp. soy sauce

1 garlic clove, crushed

Directions:

1. Place tempeh block in a sauté pan or non-stick metal skillet, cover with enough vegetable broth or water, boil over medium heat, lower the heat, simmer, about 10 minutes, drain, pat dry. Let stand to cool.

2. After being cooled, crumble into small pieces; add the tempeh, cool, about 3 minutes, stir often until it begins to turn light brown.

3. Add the flaxseeds, savory, turmeric, thyme, oregano, cayenne, and freshly ground black pepper, cook, about 3 to 4 more minutes, until lightly browned. Add a little oil as required.

4. Add the soy sauce, garlic clove to the tempeh crumbles, cook, 2 minutes more, sprinkle with crumbles to taste, cinnamon, and cardamom, remove crumbles from heat, and then serve instantly.

Green Goddess Farro Bowl

The appealing and flavorful profile of this dish will want to make you crave for more. Very easy to make. Enjoy with guests and loved ones.

Preparation Time: 20 minutes

Cooking Time: 45 minutes

Total Time: 1 hour, 5 minutes

Servings: 4

Ingredients:

For the Salad

2 cups cooked farro or quinoa

3/8 pound artichoke hearts, chopped

5/8 pound cucumber, chopped

2 1/2 ounces olives, sliced

10 ounces tomatoes, chopped

5 ounces chopped bell peppers, roasted

1/4 cup fresh mixed herbs (parsley, dill, mint, or basil)

3 tbsp. flaxseeds

1 large sliced avocado

For the baked zucchini

1 cup zucchini, sliced into rounds or sticks

1/2 cup rolled oats

3-5 tbsp. nutritional yeast

1 pressed garlic clove or diced

2 cups breadcrumbs, whole wheat

2 tsp. parsley, dried

2 tsp. oregano, dried

1/4 tbsp. sea salt

3/4 cup cornstarch, or oat flour

Dressing

1/2 medium tahini

3 tbsp. white wine

1/2 medium avocado slices

1/2 medium fresh cilantro

1/5 cup water

1/2 cup granulated garlic, or 1 minced clove garlic

Directions:

1. Preheat the oven to about 375 deg. F.

2. Cook the farro based on the directions on the package make enough for about 2 cups.

3. Add to a non-stick metal skillet, toast, over medium or low heat until lightly browned. Please be watchful to avoid burning.

4. Meanwhile, add the yeast, garlic clove, breadcrumbs, parsley, oregano, and salt to a large bowl, whisk to combine.

5. Add the cornstarch to another bowl, add rolled oats, garlic, water, pepper, and salt to a high powered blender, puree until smooth, and then, pour into another bowl.

6. Dip the round-sliced zucchini into the cornstarch, and coat gently, transfer into the blended mixture, thoroughly mix to coat, drain off excess batter.

7. Place the zucchini into the breadcrumbs mixture, press mixture into the zucchini, and then transfer onto a metallic non-stick baking pan.

8. Bake, at 375 deg. F., about 30 minutes, or until golden, turn after being half-baked about 15 minutes.

9. Meanwhile, add the tahini, white wine, avocado slices, fresh cilantro, and water, to a blender, process until creamy, sprinkle with granulated garlic, pour the mixture into 4 bowls.

10. Place the farro on the bottom of the bowl, and top around the edges with the zucchini slices, artichoke hearts, cucumbers, olives, tomatoes, and peppers.

11. Sprinkle with the flaxseeds and fresh mixed herbs, place the avocado slices in the middle, coat with the pureed dressing ingredients, serve instantly.

Cheesy Veggie Divan

The combination of cannellini beans and roasted red peppers makes this recipe a favorite for your guests! Yummy.

Preparation Time: 20 minutes

Cooking Time: 30 minutes

Total Time: 50 minutes

Servings: 6

Ingredients:

1 and 1/4 cups zucchini, thinly sliced

1/2 head cauliflower, thinly sliced

4 carrots, thinly sliced

1 chopped large onion

2 and 1/2 ounces jarred roasted red peppers, homemade

3 cups white cannellini beans drained and rinsed

3 and 1/3 tbsp. nutritional yeast

2 tsp. lemon zest, or white wine

1/2 tbsp. yellow mustard

1-ounce tahini

1/4 tbsp. dried onion

1/4 tbsp. granulated garlic

1 and 1/2 cups vegetable broth, reduced-sodium

1/4 tbsp. sea salt (optional)

Directions:

1. Apply a cooking spray on the bottom of a non-stick baking sheet.

2. Boil some water in a large pan, steam the vegetables, until crispy and softened.

3. Transfer into the prepared baking sheet.

4. Add the peppers, beans, yeast, lemon zest, yellow mustard, tahini, onion. and garlic to a high powered blender, blend, about 2-3 minutes, or until smoothened without lumps.

5. Add little vegetable broth to thin, and keep the rest, so it could be easily removed.

6. Gently scrape the cheese sauce into a large pan, heat over low or medium heat.

7. Add the remaining vegetable broth, and then thoroughly whisk to combine, until well incorporated, heat through.

8. Pour in enough sauce to cover the vegetables, turn them around a bit, and then cover with a tin foil, bake, at 350 deg. F., at least, about 25 – 30 minutes, or until well bakes, serve, topped with your favorite grain.

Banana Fried Rice with Tofu

Your family, guests, and loved ones cannot afford to resist this flavorful banana fried rice. Enjoy, topped with salad. Yummy!

Preparation Time: 30 minutes

Cooking Time: 20 minutes

Total Time: 50 minutes

Servings: 6

Ingredients:

Baked Tofu

7/8 pound organic tofu drained

2 tbsp. tomato sauce

1/8 tbsp. granulated garlic

1/4 cup soy sauce, or tamari

1/2 tsp. liquid stevia, or 4 tsp. maple syrup

1 dash hot sauce

1 tbsp. vinegar

1/8 tbsp. black pepper, dried

Fried Rice

6 tsp. chicken broth, reduced-sodium

1 medium chopped onion

1 chopped red bell pepper

1 cup peeled carrots, diced

3 garlic cloves, chopped

1 medium toasted raw cashews

3 cups brown rice, cooked

1/2 medium frozen peas, or fresh

1 cup banana, cut into bite-sized pieces

1/2 medium raisins

1/2 medium chopped cilantro

1 cup sliced green onions

Extra soy sauce, for flavor

Sauce (if desired)

2/3 medium low salt soy sauce or tamari

4 tsp. rice vinegar

4 tsp. chili garlic sauce

2 tsp. maple or date syrup

2 tsp. minced ginger

Directions:

1. Preheat the oven to about 375 deg. F. Lightly spray a metallic non-stick baking pan with cooking oil.

2. Gently wrap the drained tofu in paper towels, press, and add a large can of berries, slice into 1-inch cubes.

3. Add the tomato sauce, granulated garlic, soy sauce, liquid stevia or maple syrup, hot sauce, vinegar, and black pepper to a large mixing bowl, stir until well incorporated.

4. Gently whisk in tofu cubes into the sauce, marinate, about 10 minutes or more.

5. Place the tofu cubes mixture on the baking sheet on a single layer, bake, about 15 minutes, and then turn the tofu, bake until browned on the other side too, additional 15 minutes.

6. Pour the chicken broth into a large pan, sauté the onions, red bell pepper, peeled carrots, garlic cloves, about 3-4 minutes, or until tender but firm.

7. Add the toasted raw cashews, sauté, about 30 seconds more.

8. Add the brown rice, stir, fry, a few minutes, and then add the banana slices, frozen peas, and raisins, whisk in the baked tofu.

9. Remove from the heat, if desired, top with soy sauce, chili garlic sauce, rice vinegar, minced ginger, and maple syrup; serve topped with cilantro and green onions.

Baked Spaghetti and Cheese

The combination of veggies and roasted red peppers make it healthy and delicious. Enjoy with guests!

Preparation Time: 20 minutes

Cooking Time: 25 minutes

Total Time: 45 minutes

Servings: 6

Ingredients:

1 package spaghetti pasta

1/2 medium raw cashews, soaked in hot water 30 minutes

1 1/2 cups plain yogurt

3 whole roasted red bell peppers

4 tbsp. nutritional yeast

3/8 tbsp. granulated garlic

1/4 tbsp. dried onion

1 tbsp. light miso

1/2 cup buttermilk

4 tsp. Dijon mustard

1/8 tbsp. dried black pepper

1/4 tbsp. salt

4 tsp. all-purpose flour

Dash cayenne pepper

Cashew Parmesan Cheese

2 and 1/2 ounces raw cashews

4 tsp. nutritional yeast

1/6 tbsp. salt

Directions:

1. Preheat the oven to about 350 deg. F., cook the spaghetti pasta based on the directions on the package.

2. Remove from heat, rinse, drain, and then transfer into a large baking sheet.

3. Add all the ingredients to a high powered blender, blend until smoothened.

4. Pour the pureed sauce into a large saucepan, heat over medium or low heat, stir continuously until the cheese sauce becomes thick.

5. Pour the thickened cheese sauce over the cooked spaghetti pasta.

6. To prepare the parmesan cheese, add all the ingredients to a blender, blend until crumbly.

7. Cook, about 25 minutes, or until it bubbles, and the round edges begin browning.

Classic Basil Marinara with Angel Hair Pasta

This super tasty dish is very easy to prepare in just minutes. It is a very nice plus to your recipe collections. Yummy!

Preparation Time: 15 minutes

Cooking Time: 15 minutes

Total Time: 30 minutes

Servings: 4

Ingredients:

16 ounces angel hair pasta whole wheat

1/4 cup water

1/2 cup diced onion

1/2 cup diced carrot

4 minced garlic cloves

1 sliced garlic clove

5 and 3/5 cups whole tomatoes

1/2 tsp. red pepper flakes

1/2 tbsp. basil, dried

10 fresh leaves & fresh julienned basil

1 tbsp. corn syrup

1/2 tsp. sea salt and pepper, or to taste

Directions:

1. Pour about a 1/4 cup of water into a sauté pan, sauté the onion, add the carrot, and garlic cloves, cook, about 3-4 minutes or until softened.

2. Process the whole tomatoes, red pepper flakes, and basil in a food processor or high immersion blender.

3. Add the corn syrup, salt, and pepper. Boil; lower the heat, sauté, while partly covered, about 20 minutes.

4. Stir in fresh basil; cook the pasta according to the directions on the package.

5. Drain, add the cooked pasta to the pan, toss very well to coat with the sauce. Serve immediately.

Pasta Puttanesca with Spanish Olives
Enjoy this delicious meal while your mind flashes back to yummy supreme dough-less pizza.

Preparation Time: 20 minutes

Cooking Time: 30 minutes

Total Time: 50 minutes

Servings: 4

Ingredients:

1/2 pound vermicelli pasta whole grain

1/4 cup water

1/2 cup red onion, chopped

1/3 cup seedless Spanish olives, sliced if large

1/2 jar marinara sauce

1/2 cup sun-dried tomatoes sliced

4 cups fresh baby spinach

3 cups tomatoes, diced

3 large garlic cloves, sliced

2/3 medium chopped parsley

1/2 tsp. salt, or to taste

1/2 tsp. pepper, or to taste

Directions:

1. Boil water in a large pot, add the vermicelli pasta, cook based on the package directions.

2. Meanwhile, heat a large metallic skillet, sauté the red onion until softened, evaporated.

3. Add the olives, marinara sauce, sun-dried tomatoes, baby spinach, and diced tomatoes.

4. Whisk in the sliced garlic cloves and parsley until well combined, sauté until thoroughly cooked.

5. Transfer the cooked pasta to a serving dish, and gently toss to combine. Enjoy with guests.

Tamale Pie

You would want to share this flavorful and tasty meal with your friends. Yummy!

Preparation Time: 30 minutes

Cooking Time: 45 minutes

Total Time: 1 hour, 15 minutes

Servings: 8

Ingredients:

1 large green bell pepper, diced

1 large onion, diced

4 minced garlic cloves

1 tbsp. Ancho chili powder

1 tbsp. paprika, smoked

1 tbsp. cumin, ground

1 tbsp. dried oregano

1 and 1/2 cups diced fire-roasted tomatoes with juice

2 4 oz. cans diced green chilies with juice

1 and 1/2 cups low sodium black beans rinsed and drained

1 and 1/2 cups low-salt pinto beans rinsed and drained

1/2 tsp. pepper, or to taste

1/2 tsp. sea salt, or to taste

1 medium chopped cilantro

Masa Layer

3 masa harina

1/4 tsp. baking soda

1/2 tsp. cream of tartar

1/4 tbsp. sea salt, or to taste

3/4 cup applesauce

1 and 1/2 cups low sodium vegetable broth

1 and 1/2 cups water

Directions:

1. Preheat the oven to about 350 deg. F., spray a large baking pan with cooking oil.

2. Over a medium or high, heat about 2 tablespoons water in a Dutch oven, add the green bell pepper and onion, sauté for 3 minutes.

3. Frequently stir to prevent burning, until the onions are softened, if the pan begins drying out, add some water, and then add the cloves garlic, sauté some few more minutes.

4. In a bowl, thoroughly whisk the chili powder, paprika, cumin, and oregano, and then stir in the spices mixture until well mixed, lower the heat if the need arises.

5. Add the tomatoes, green chilies, and beans, whisk to combine, and then sprinkle pepper and salt.

6. Keep cooking until the mixture turns a bit watery, whisk in the chopped cilantro, and then remove from the heat.

7. Meanwhile, fill your baking sheet with the filling mixture.

To prepare the masa layer,

8. Stir all the ingredients in a mixing bowl until well combined, and should be like the consistency of a thickened pancake mixture.

9. Carefully spread the masa mixture over the filling mixture using a large spoon.

10. Bake, at 350 deg. F., about 45 minutes, or until the topping begins turning brown, and doesn't turn soft again, and then serve with the toppings instantly.

Quinoa With Stuffed Peppers

Your guests will prefer having this colorful dish at lunch or dinner. Tasty!

Preparation Time: 25 minutes

Cooking Time: 30 minutes

Total Time: 55 minutes

Servings: 4

Ingredients:

1 and 1/2 cups quinoa, cooked

3 large deseeded red peppers, sliced in half lengthwise

1/2 cup onion, chopped

1 and 3/5 cups sliced mushrooms

2 chopped garlic cloves

1 and 1/2 cups rinsed kidney beans, drained

8 roughly chopped tomatoes, sun-dried, soaked in hot water

2-3 large Swiss chard leaves, roughly chopped

1 and 1/2 cups tomato ketchup

2/3 medium raw cashews, finely chopped

Directions:

1. Preheat the oven to 375 deg. F.

2. Parboil the peppers in boiling water, about 5 minutes.

3. In a large sauté pan, add a little water sauté the onions over medium heat, add mushrooms and garlic, continue cooking until the veggies turn softened.

4. Add the Swiss chard leaves and beans, sauté until wilted.

5. Whisk in the tomato ketchup, sun-dried tomatoes, and 1 and 1/2 cups quinoa.

6. Fill up the cups, and then top with the chopped cashews, cook, covered with a tin foil, about 20 to 25 minutes, or until wilted through. Remove the foil, cook, about 5 to 10 minutes more, or until the cashews are browned. Let stand to cool, serve instantly.

Curried Chickpea Rice Salad

You can get this flavorful, energetic, and tasty recipe prepared in a very easy way; just great for lunch or dinner.

Preparation Time: 20 minutes

Cooking Time: 1 hour

Total Time: 1 hour, 20 minutes

Servings: 6

Ingredients:

Baked Tofu

2 and 1/2 tbsp. tamari

1/5 cup rice vinegar

2 tbsp. tomato ketchup

1 tbsp. hot sauce

3/4 tbsp. liquid stevia

1/8 tbsp. granulated garlic

1/4 tsp. black pepper, ground

14 oz. drained organic tofu, sliced into 1-inch cubes

Rice Salad

2 cups brown rice, cooked

1/2 cup rinsed chickpeas, drained

1 and 1/3 medium chopped red onion

1 chopped red bell pepper cored, seeded

1 medium raisin, seedless

1/2 tbsp. cumin, ground

1 cup chopped parsley

Dressing:

1/5 cup apple cider vinegar

2 tbsp. lemon juice

2 tbsp. red curry paste

2 tbsp. maple syrup

1/4 tbsp. sea salt, or to taste

Directions:

1. Preheat the oven to about 375 deg. F., and then spray gently, a baking sheet with cooking oil.

2. Whisk the tamari, rice vinegar, tomato ketchup, hot sauce, liquid stevia, granulated garlic, and black pepper in a small mixing bowl.

3. Carefully stir in the tofu cubes, cover, marinate, about 10 minutes.

4. In one layer, add the marinated tofu on the baking sheet, bake, at 375 deg. F., about 15 minutes. Turn the tofu, baking 15 more minutes, or until browned.

5. For the rice salad, add the vinegar, maple syrup, lemon juice, curry powder and salt to a large mixing bowl, thoroughly whisk to combine.

6. In another bowl, add the cooked rice, chickpeas, onion, bell pepper, raisins, dried cumin, chopped parsley, and onion, thoroughly coat to mix.

7. Pour in the dressing, and then thoroughly mix, serve instantly.

Instant Pot White Bean Soup with Garlic, Mushrooms, and Quinoa

You would discover how amazing it is to get this easy, delicious, and super nutritious soup prepared. In less than 30 minutes, it's ready. Yummy!

Preparation Time: 20 minutes

Cooking Time: 22 minutes

Total Time: 44 minutes

Servings: 8

Ingredients:

1 and 1/2 cups dry cannellini beans rinsed and picked over for small stones or debris

1 cup quinoa

1/2 cup chopped onion

3 cups sliced mushrooms

8 garlic cloves, finely chopped

1/2 jalapeño pepper seeds removed and finely chopped

1/5 cup Thai red curry paste

1 chopped shallot

2 tsp. Braggs Liquid Amino (if desired)

10 cups homemade vegetable broth, or store-bought

1 and 1/2 cups tomato ketchup

1/2 tsp. pepper, or to taste

1/2 tsp. Salt, or to taste

Garnish

1/4 cup chopped parsley

1/4 cup chopped scallions

1/4 cup low-fat yogurt (optional)

Directions:

1. Set aside the tomato ketchup, chopped scallions, and parsley, and then add the remaining ingredients to the instant pot.

2. Set the pot on manual, high pressure, cook, about 22 minutes. You could turn on the pot, an additional 5 to 7 minutes if the beans are soft.

3. Using the quick-release method, hit 'pressure', and then let sit, about 10 to 15 minutes on the 'keep warm' setting.

4. Whisk in the tomato ketchup, sprinkle pepper and salt to taste, and then serve, topped with parsley and scallions. And if you like, add low-fat yogurt.

Easy Plant-Based Vegetable Broth

Make your soups flavorful while sautéing veggies with this low salt vegetable broth. Your family will love the taste. Yummy!

Preparation Time: 15 minutes

Cooking Time: 30 minutes

Total Time: 45 minutes

Servings: 10

Ingredients:

1 large onion

5 chopped stalks celery

3 large unpeeled carrots

1/3 head broccoli, cut into large chunks

4 garlic cloves

3 cups roughly chopped greens

2 tomatoes, sliced into large chunks

1/2 bunch cilantro

1/4 pound mushrooms, cut in half

2 bay leaves

1/2 tbsp. black peppercorns

1/4 tbsp. sea salt (if desired)

10 cups water

Directions:

1. Pour 10 cups water into an instant pot; add all the ingredients, close the lid, pressure cook, on high, about 15 minutes.

2. Release the remaining pressure, 15 minutes, using natural release, by switching the knob to the venting position.

3. Carefully open the lid, strain the broth through a large colander into a bowl.

4. Keep in a tight container, or place in the refrigerator to freeze. If you are using the stovetop, chop the veggies into large chunks.

5. Sauté the onions over medium heat in a large pot, about 2 minutes, or until fragrant, add the garlic cloves, salt (if using), cook 30 minutes more.

6. Add the remaining ingredients into the pot, boil, carefully whisk to combine, simmer, covered, on low, about 1 hour. It becomes more concentrated as you simmer.

7. Remove the larger pieces by carefully straining the broth via a large colander, and remove the rest through a fine-mesh strainer.

8. Keep in a tight container, or place in the fridge.

Spring Asparagus, Pea, Zucchini Soup with Pesto

This is a fast, easy meal that stands as a favorite to your guests. Yummy!

Preparation Time: 15 minutes

Cooking Time: 15 minutes

Total Time: 30 minutes

Servings: 6

Ingredients:

1/4 cup water

2 garlic cloves, chopped

1/2 cup onion, chopped

1 bunch asparagus

2 medium peas

5 cups vegetable broth, low sodium

1 and 1/2 cups sliced zucchini

1 cup buttermilk

1/2 lime juice

1/2 tbsp. sea salt

1/8 tbsp. pepper

Pesto

1 and 1/2 cups tightly packed fresh basil leaves

1/2 cup chopped cilantro or tightly packed parsley

3 garlic cloves

2 tsp. light miso red

3 tbsp. nutritional yeast

1/4 medium pine nuts

3 tbsp. lemon zest

1/2 tsp. sea salt, or to taste

1/2 tsp. pepper, or to taste

Directions:

1. Add 1/4 cup of water to a large soup pot, over medium or low heat, sauté the garlic cloves and onion, about a minute, or until fragrant.

2. Chop off rough ends of the asparagus, cut into an inch size, transfer into the pot, add the peas, vegetable broth, zucchini, and buttermilk.

3. Cook, covered, on medium heat, about 25 minutes, or until the asparagus turns softened.

4. Let stand to cool, about 8 to 10 minutes, add the lime juice, pepper, and salt to taste, and then transfer to a blender, blend thoroughly in batches, until well smoothened, creamy, and without lumps.

5. Pour mixture back into the soup pot, serve the soup into 6 serving bowls, top with a dollop of pesto.

Vegetable Soup with Buckwheat

This veggie soup recipe contains spinach, romaine lettuce, creamy cannellini beans, and more. You could replace brown rice with buckwheat for a more chewy bite. Yummy!

Preparation Time: 20 minutes

Cooking Time: 30 minutes

Total Time: 50 minutes

Servings: 12

Ingredients:

2 and 1/2 cups vegetable broth, low sodium

2 inches leeks cut in half and then a 1/4-inch slices

1/2 pound chopped potatoes

4 celery stalks, chopped

3 chopped carrots

4 garlic cloves, minced

1 chopped yellow onion

1/4 tbsp ground pepper, or to taste

1/2 tbsp. sea salt, or to taste

1 cup buckwheat

12 cups romaine lettuce, diced

2 cups chopped spinach, fresh or frozen,

15 oz. cannellini beans with liquid

2 10-oz.can tomatoes with liquid, diced

10 oz. sweet corn with liquid

3/4 tbsp. tarragon, dried

2 tsp. thyme, fresh

1/2 tbsp. coriander, dried

1/4 tbsp. celery seed

1/4 tbsp. saffron or turmeric

Directions:

1. In a large pot, sauté a 1/4 cup of the vegetable broth, and set the remaining aside for further use.

2. Add the leeks, potatoes, celery stalks, carrots, garlic cloves, onion, pepper, and salt to taste, stir, sauté until the onions are tender.

3. Add the remaining 2 and 1/4 vegetable broth, buckwheat, romaine lettuce, spinach, cannellini beans, tomatoes, sweet corn, and all the spices.

4. Cook, on low heat, about 30 minutes, or until cooked through, let stand to cool, serve instantly.

Tomato, Carrot, Brussels Sprouts Soup

Enjoy this heart-healthy, tasty, delicious soup recipe with your family. The addition of carrot juice and Brussels sprouts makes the taste so unique. Yummy!

Preparation Time: 25 minutes

Cooking Time: 30 minutes

Total Time: 55 minutes

Servings: 6

Ingredients:

1/4 cup water

1/2 cup yellow onion, chopped

5 garlic cloves, minced

1/4 tbsp. garam masala

1/6 tbsp. Ceylon cinnamon

2 peeled carrots, and cut into rounds

3 cups Brussels sprouts, cut into 1/4-inch cubes

1 large beet, peeled, cut into 1/2-inch cubes

2/3 medium green lentils, uncooked

1 medium red lentil, uncooked

4 cups vegetable broth

1 and 3/5 cups tomato ketchup

1/2 cup kidney beans canned no salt

2 cups carrot juice

4 tsp. peanut butter or almond

1/2 tsp. salt, or to taste

1/2 tsp. pepper, or to taste

Directions:

1. Add about a 1/4 cup of water to a large pot, over medium heat, sauté the garlic cloves, and yellow onion, until soft and translucent.

2. Whisk in the garam masala and Ceylon cinnamon, Brussels sprouts, and beet sauté a few more minutes.

3. Add the green and red lentils, vegetable broth, tomato ketchup, kidney beans, carrot juice, and peanut butter.

4. Cook, covered, about 30 to 45 minutes, or until the veggies turn crispy, softened, and the green and red lentils are softened as well.

5. Sprinkle salt and pepper to taste, and then serve at warm or room temperature.

Vegan Corn Chowder

Aiming at serving a large crowd at your next party? Your guests would gain interest in this flavorful, comforting, creamy vegan corn chowder! Yummy!

Preparation Time: 20 minutes

Cooking Time: 30 minutes

Total Time: 50 minutes

Servings: 8

Ingredients:

1/4 cup water

1 cup yellow onion, chopped finely

2 garlic cloves, minced

2 celery ribs, chopped

1 cup red bell pepper seeded and chopped

1/4 tbsp. red pepper flakes (if desired)

1/2 cup peeled potato, diced

1 cup plain yogurt

2 cups vegetable broth, low sodium

1 tbsp. cumin, ground

1 tbsp. Ancho chili powder

1 tbsp. oregano, dried

1 tbsp. cinnamon, dried

1 tbsp. paprika, smoked

4 tsp. yeast (if desired)

1/2 cup lemon zest

2 cups fresh corn kernels, or frozen

1/4 tbsp. salt, or to taste

1/2 tsp. pepper, or to taste

Garnish

fresh cilantro, or parsley

green onion chopped

1/4 cup red pepper, chopped

Directions:

161

1. Sauté the yellow onion, garlic cloves, celery ribs, and 3/4 cup red bell pepper, and red pepper flakes (if using) in a large pot of water containing 1/4 cup water, sauté, about 8 to 10 minutes, or until the vegetables are tender.

2. Stir in the diced potato, plain yogurt, and veggie broth.

3. Whisk the spices (cumin, chili powder, oregano, cinnamon, and paprika) in a mixing bowl, pour spices mixture into the pot.

4. Add the yeast (if using), lemon zest, thoroughly stir until well combined and then boil, lower the heat, cook, covered with a lid, about 18 to 20 minutes, or until the potatoes are fork-tender.

5. Add the corn kernels, stir to mix, cook, 8 to 10 more minutes, or until corn is softened to your taste. Let stand to cool, about 10 minutes.

6. Once cooled, transfer 1/3 of the soup to a blender, blend until smoothened without lumps.

7. Pour back the blended soup into the pot, thoroughly stir, and then sprinkle salt and pepper to taste, let stand to cool, and then serve, topped with fresh cilantro or parsley, chopped green onion and 1/4 cup rep pepper.

Sauerkraut Soup

This sauerkraut soup is easily prepared in a matter of minutes and would help you boost your immunity. Enjoy with your family!

Preparation Time: 20 minutes

Cooking Time: 25 minutes

Total Time: 45 minutes

Servings: 8

Ingredients:

1/4 cup water

1/2 cup diced onion

1 rib celery, finely diced

1 cup carrots, thinly sliced

1/2 medium uncooked farro, rinsed

1 and 1/2 cups potatoes peeled, cut in 1/2-inch cubes

1 bay leaf

8 cups vegetable broth, low sodium

2 cups of water

1 and 1/2 cups cannellini beans drained and rinsed

2-3 cups rinsed sauerkraut, drained

1/2 tsp. salt, or to taste

1/2 tsp. pepper, or to taste

Directions:

1. Sauté the onion and celery in a 1/4 cup of water over medium heat, about 5 minutes, or until tender and light brown.

2. Stir in the carrots, farro, potatoes, bay leaf, vegetable broth, and water, boil on high, lower the heat, simmer, about 13 to 15 minutes, or until the veggies are soft.

3. Add the cannellini beans with juice, rinsed sauerkraut, simmer, about 10 more minutes, remove the bay leaf, let stand to cool.

4. Transfer a 1/2 of the cooled soup into a high powered blender, thoroughly blend soup until smoothened, and then pour the blended soup into the other 1/2 soup, thoroughly stir until incorporated.

5. Sprinkle salt and pepper to taste and then serve the soup into 8 bowls.

Vichyssoise with Fennel

With the combination of cashews and unsweetened almond milk, this vichyssoise soup will make you healthy and very active. Tasty!

Preparation Time: 15 minutes

Cooking Time: 10 minutes

Total Time: 25 minutes

Servings: 6

Ingredients:

1 and 1/2 cups potatoes, Yukon gold

1 cup fennel bulbs, washed

1/2 yellow onion, chopped or 3 large leeks

3 garlic cloves, chopped

1 and 1/2 cups low sodium vegetable broth

1 sprig thyme

1 medium raw cashews, soaked in hot water (if desired)

1/2 cup vinegar (if desired)

1 and 1/2 cups unsweetened almond milk

Directions:

1. Turn on the sauté function in your pressure cooker, add the fennel bulbs and yellow onion, sauté until softened.

2. Meanwhile, chop the potatoes, and add to the pressure cooker.

3. Add the garlic cloves, vegetable broth, thyme, raw cashews (if using), and vinegar (if using).

4. Set for 10 minutes using the manual settings of the pressure cooker, and the timer begins after warming up.

5. Manually cool or gently release the pressure with the valve once the timing is concluded.

6. Blend the soup with a high powered blender, about 10 minutes, or until smoothened.

7. Add the unsweetened almond milk, stir to mix thoroughly, and then serve, topped with chopped green onion.

Slow Cooker Spices Soup with Spinach

Coat in all the ingredients into your slow cooker and soonest, your soup is ready and you can't wait to get it served. Yummy!

Preparation Time: 20 minutes

Cooking Time: 4 hours

Total Time: 4 hours, 20 minutes

Servings: 6

Ingredients:

2 garlic cloves, minced

3 large leeks, or 1 small yellow onion

1 and 1/4 cups tomato sauce

1 and 1/4 cups tomato ketchup

2 large carrots, sliced

2 small red potatoes, cut into 1/2" cubes

1 and 1/2 cups pinto beans drained and rinsed low salt

2 ribs celery, sliced

1 large green bell pepper, chopped

3 cups vegetable broth, low sodium

1/2 tbsp. cinnamon, dried

1/2 tbsp. basil, dried

1 tbsp. oregano, dried

1/2 tsp. salt

1/2 tsp. pepper, or to taste

3/4 cup buckwheat, uncooked

2-3 cups fresh spinach, packed

Directions:

1. Add the garlic cloves, leeks, tomatoes (sauce and ketchup), sliced carrots, red potatoes, low salt pinto beans, sliced celery, green bell pepper, and vegetable broth to a large slow cooker.

2. Add in the cinnamon, basil, and oregano, and then sprinkle salt and pepper to taste, or leave out salt completely.

3. Cook, on low heat, about 8 hours, or on high, about 4 hours, add the uncooked buckwheat, cook, about 18 to 20 more minutes, or until the buckwheat is well cooked.

4. Carefully stir in fresh spinach, add seasonings to your taste, enjoy with your guests.

Mulligatawny Soup

You would feel the mouth-watering smell of this Indian-spiced soup while cooking it in your kitchen. You are about to cut down calorie to the barest minimum. Tastes nice!

Preparation Time: 20 minutes

Cooking Time: 30 minutes

Total Time: 50 minutes

Servings: 6

Ingredients:

1/4 cup water

1 large yellow onion, chopped, or 4 large leeks

1 large carrot peeled and diced

2 small or 1 large potato peeled and diced

1 large firm apple peeled, cored and diced

1 tbsp. fresh ginger, peeled and minced

3 garlic cloves, minced

1 and 1/2 cups diced tomatoes

1 tbsp. red curry paste

1/4 tbsp. ground cinnamon

1/4 tbsp. ground cardamom

1/4 tbsp. ground coriander

1/4 tbsp. ground turmeric

1/8 tbsp. freshly ground black pepper

2 medium uncooked red lentils, rinsed and cleaned

4 cups low sodium vegetable broth

2/3 cup non-dairy milk

1/2 tbsp. coconut extract

1/2 tsp. salt, or to taste

1/2 tsp. pepper, or to taste

For garnish:

1/3 cup cilantro chopped, and/or

1/3 cup scallions

Directions:

1. Pour the 1/4 cup water into a large soup pot, add the yellow onion, and carrot, sauté over medium or low heat, about 4 to 5 minutes, or until the onions are softened.

2. Add the potatoes, apples, fresh ginger, garlic cloves, and tomatoes, sauté, 3 more minutes.

3. Stir in red curry paste, cinnamon, cardamom, coriander, turmeric, and black pepper, thoroughly whisk to coat.

4. Pour the vegetable broth into the pot, and then add the red lentils, bring to a boil on high, once boiled, lower the heat, simmer, uncovered, about 30 minutes.

5. You may add some more water if it's too thick. Let stand to cool.

6. Pour 1/2 of the soup into a high powered blender, thoroughly blend until smoothened without lumps, and then pour back into the soup pot, thoroughly stir.

7. Whisk in the milk and coconut extract, cook, a few more minutes, sprinkle salt and pepper to taste, and then serve, topped with crusty bread, scallions, cilantro, or parsley.

Winter Immunity Mushroom Soup

Within 20 to 30 minutes, your mushroom soup is made. You want to get the best from the addition of kidney beans to boost your vitality. Yummy!

Preparation Time: 15 minutes

Cooking Time: 20 minutes

Total Time: 35 minutes

Servings: 6

Ingredients:

1/8 cup water

1 large yellow sweet onion, chopped

1/2 cup red onion, chopped

4 garlic cloves, chopped

1 and 3/5 cups mushrooms, sliced

4 cups vegetable broth, low sodium

1/2 cup coconut milk

1 tbsp. herbal mushroom powder (if desired)

1 and 1/2 cups rinsed kidney beans, drained, low sodium

1/2 tsp. salt, or to taste

1/2 tsp. pepper, or to taste

Directions:

1. Add 1/8 cup of water to a large pot, over medium heat, sauté the onions, and garlic cloves, about 8 to 10 minutes, or until softened and fragrant.

2. Add the sliced mushrooms, cook, covered, on low heat, about 10 to 15minutes, or until the mushrooms are halved in size. Let stand to cool.

3. Once cooled, transfer half-cooked mushrooms, 1 and 1/2 cups vegetable broth, and coconut milk into a high powered blender, thoroughly blend at high speed, about 5 minutes, or until crispy and smoothened without lumps.

4. You could sprinkle the herbal mushroom powder if you wish.

5. Pour back the blended soup into the pot, add the kidney beans, cook, about 5 to 10 more minutes.

6. Sprinkle pepper and salt to taste if desired, serve the soup into 6 serving bowls and enjoy.

Black Bean Soup

A hot bowl of soup is great when it's very cold. Sweet potato makes this soup very rich, and you can't afford to resist the taste! Yummy!

Preparation Time: 15 minutes

Cooking Time: 30 minutes

Total Time: 45 minutes

Servings: 8

Ingredients:

1/4 cup water

1 large onion, diced

2 ribs celery, diced

1 large seeded red bell pepper, diced

1 large sweet potato, peeled, cut into 1/2" cubes

3 cups low sodium black beans rinsed and drained

1/4 cup low sodium vegetable broth

2 cups of water

1/2 tbsp. ground cumin

1/4 tbsp. ground coriander

1/4 tbsp. sea salt or to taste

1/6 tbsp. ground pepper

1 large avocado, diced

1 tbsp. chervil, chopped

1/3 cup mayonnaise (if desired)

Directions:

1. Add about 1/4 cup water to a large pot, sauté the diced onion, ribs celery, red bell pepper, and potato over medium or low heat, until tender.

2. Add the black beans to the pot, pour in about 2 cups of water, together with the vegetable broth.

3. Add the coriander, cumin, and then sprinkle pepper, and salt.

4. Cook, covered, on medium heat, about 30 minutes, or until the vegetables and potatoes are fork-tender.

5. Let stand to cool, transfer half of the soup into a high powered blender, blend until smoothened.

6. Pour the blended soup back into the pot, thoroughly stir, and then serve, topped with avocado, sprinkle chopped chervil or minced cilantro. And you may wish to add a dollop of mayonnaise or sour cream.

Pressure Cooker Black Beans

You can have beans to use in salsa, salads, or casseroles in just 20 minutes. What a great collection to your plant-based recipes! Yummy!

Preparation Time: 10 minutes

Cooking Time: 20 minutes

Total Time: 30 minutes

Servings: 8

Ingredients:

3 cups black beans, dried

7 cups of water

1/2 peeled onion, chopped

3 garlic cloves, crushed

2 bay leaves

Directions:

1. Carefully pick over, and rinse the black beans, add to the pressure cooker.

2. Add about 7 cups water, add the chopped onion, garlic cloves, and bay leaves.

3. Cover set pressure on high, 20 to 25 minutes. You could also soak the beans all through the night if you would prefer a more quick method, if you do, it will be cooked in just about 8 to 10 minutes.

4. For the quick soak method, boil about 7 cups of water in a large pot, and then add the black beans, bring to a boil for just about 2 minutes.

5. Remove from the stove, let sit for 1 hour, continue with the recipe (about 10 minutes cooking time), and then serve at warm or room temperature.

Hearty Lentil Soup with Spinach

This lentil soup is very easy to make. The combination of spinach and potatoes makes it tasty! Yummy!

Preparation Time: 30 minutes

Cooking Time: 30 minutes

Total Time: 1 hour

Servings: 6

Ingredients:

1/4 cup water

1/2 cup large onion, chopped

2 celery stalks, chopped

3 garlic cloves, peeled and minced

1 and 1/2 cups peeled carrots, chopped

4 cups vegetable broth, low sodium

6 tbsp. tomato ketchup

2 cups regular brown lentils, cooked

1 large potato peeled and chopped

1/4 tbsp. coriander

1/4 tbsp. cumin

1/4 tbsp. sea salt, or to taste

1/8 tbsp. pepper, freshly ground

2-3 cups fresh spinach, packed

Directions:

1. Add a 1/4 cup water into a large pot, over medium heat, sauté the onion, celery stalks, garlic cloves, and peeled carrots, for some minutes, or until they begin to get tender.

2. Stir in the vegetable broth and tomato ketchup.

3. Add the lentils, potato, and then whisk in the spices (coriander, cumin), sprinkle pepper and salt taste, cook, covered, on medium heat, about 20 minutes.

4. Add the fresh spinach, stir, cook, about 12 to 20 more minutes, or until the spinach and lentils are tender.

Roasted Cauliflower Chowder

Without any dairy, you can get the best of satisfaction from this cauliflower chowder soup with just the combination of carrot, chickpeas, cashews, potatoes, and leeks, simply for its healthy, tasty, and nutritious creamy consistency! Yummy!

Preparation Time: 30 minutes

Cooking Time: 10 minutes

Total Time: 40 minutes

Servings: 4

Ingredients:

1 medium raw cashews, soaked in hot water for at least an hour

1 head cauliflower florets, chopped

1 pound potato, peeled, cut into 1/4-inch cubes

2 large carrots, peeled, chopped

1/2 tbsp. sea salt, or to taste

1/4 tbsp. ground pepper

2 large leeks, or 1/2 cup chopped yellow onion

1 bulb garlic, top sliced off

1 medium chickpea, no salt added

4 cups low sodium vegetable broth

1/4 cup nutritional yeast

1/4 cup vinegar

1/6 tbsp. Tabasco

Directions:

1. Soak the raw cashews in a bowl with hot water, at least an hour.

2. Meanwhile, preheat the oven to about 425 deg. F., line up a baking sheet with a tin foil, add the cauliflower florets, potatoes, carrots, sprinkle pepper and salt.

3. Wrap the garlic bulb in a tin foil, add to the baking sheet.

4. Roast, at 425 deg. F., about 20 to 25 minutes, or until the cauliflower begins turning brown and the vegetables are fork-tender.

5. Wait for the veggies to cool, and then add them to a high powered blender, squeeze out the garlic off its skin, and add to the blender.

6. Add the hot water soaked cashew (now cooled), yeast, and chickpeas to the blender, pour in the vegetable broth, Tabasco, and vinegar, thoroughly blend until smoothened, creamy, and without lumps.

7. Taste and adjust the seasonings as preferred, transfer into a large pot, cook to heat through, add more water to thin if required, let stand to cool, and then serve instantly.

Easy Chana Masala With Chickpeas & Yams

Enjoy this 1-pot tasty, flavorful, healthy, and popular Indian dish with your loved ones. Yummy!

Preparation Time: 10 minutes

Cooking Time: 30 minutes

Total Time: 40 minutes

Servings: 4

Ingredients:

1/4 cup vegetable broth

5 garlic cloves, minced

1 tbsp. ginger, minced

1 red diced onion

1/2 tbsp. cumin, ground

1/8 tsp. Tabasco, or cayenne pepper

2 tsp. red curry paste

1/2 tbsp. coriander

1/2 tbsp. paprika

1 tbsp. garam masala

1/2 tbsp. sea salt, or to taste

3 tbsp. tomato ketchup

1/4 tbsp. coconut extract

3/4 cup plain yogurt

1 1/2 cups rinsed chickpeas, drained

1 1/2 cup frozen peas

2 small potatoes, chopped

1 3/4 cups tomatoes, diced

Directions:

1. Add about 1/4 vegetable broth to a large soup pot, over medium heat, sauté the garlic cloves, ginger, and onions, about 5 minutes, or until tender, and liquid almost evaporated.

2. In a mixing bowl, add the cumin, Tabasco or cayenne pepper, red curry paste, coriander, paprika, garam masala, and salt to taste, thoroughly stir to combine.

3. Transfer the spices mixture onto the sautéed vegetables, cook, 1 more minute, add the tomato ketchup.

4. Whisk the coconut extract and plain yogurt together in a mixing bowl, pour over the veggies, stir to combine.

5. Add the chickpeas, peas, potatoes, and diced tomatoes with the juice, cover, simmer, about 25 minutes, or until the potatoes are fork-tender.

6. Let stand to cool, serve, topped with mango chutney, bananas, or raisins.

Irish Cabbage Potato Soup with Dumplings

You can serve this Irish cabbage soup straight from the pot after cooking the whole wheat dumplings. Tasty and delicious!

Preparation Time: 25 minutes

Cooking Time: 30 minutes

Total Time: 55 minutes

Servings: 6

Ingredients:

1/4 cup vegetable broth, low sodium

1/2 cup chopped onion

3 garlic cloves, crushed

1/2 sliced green cabbage

1 cup peeled potatoes, chopped

4 peeled carrots, chopped

1 bay leaf

1/4 tbsp. fresh thyme

4 tsp. nutritional yeast (if desired)

6 cups vegetable broth, low sodium

1/2 tsp. sea salt, or to taste

1/2 tsp. black pepper, or to taste

Dumplings

1 cup whole wheat flour

1 tbsp. baking powder

1/2 tsp. sea salt (if desired)

1/2 tbsp. Rosemary, dried

1/2 cup cornstarch

3/4 cup almond milk, unsweetened

Directions:

1. Pour about a 1/4 cup vegetable broth into the pressure cooker, hit the 'sauté' button, add the onion, cook, stir, until they start turning soft.

2. Add garlic, keep sautéing, a few more minutes, and then add the remaining ingredients, cook, covered with the lid, about 20 minutes.

3. Meanwhile, mix all of the dumpling ingredients in a bowl, after the time is done, and at reduced pressure, gently open

the pot, sprinkle some black pepper to taste, and if required, adjust the salt to your preference.

4. Bring the soup back to a boil by hitting the 'sauté' button, so the dumplings could be well cooked.

5. Add 1 tablespoonful of the dumpling mixture into the boiling soup.

6. Boil, on medium or high heat, about 6 to 10 minutes, flip them halfway through. Let stand to cool, and then serve.

Moroccan Stew with Spinach

You are about to get a touch of sweetness from dried apricots with this stew, enriched with spinach, lentils, and full chickpeas. Yummy!

Preparation Time: 30 minutes

Cooking Time: 30 minutes

Total Time: 1 hour

Servings: 6

Ingredients:

1/4 cup water

1 large sweet onion chopped

1 tbsp. ground cumin

1/4 tbsp. ground cloves

1 tbsp. parsley, dried

1/4 tbsp. ground nutmeg

1/4 tbsp. curry powder

1/2 tbsp. ground ginger

1/4 tbsp. ground turmeric

1 tsp. sea salt, or to taste

4 cups vegetable broth, low sodium

4 large carrots, chopped

1 cup sweet peeled potatoes, chopped

3 large peeled potatoes, chopped

1 1/2 cups garbanzo beans, drained

1 1/2 cups diced tomatoes, non-drained

5/8 pound dried lentils, rinsed

1 medium chopped apricots, dried

2 cups fresh spinach, packed

1/2 tsp. sea salt, or to taste

1/2 tsp. pepper, or to taste

Directions:

1. Add 1/4 cup water to a large pot, over medium heat; cook the onion, about 5-10 minutes, or until tender.

2. In a large mixing bowl, add the cumin, cloves, parsley, nutmeg, curry powder, ginger, turmeric, thoroughly whisk to combine.

3. Whisk in the spices mixture, cook about 2 more minutes, or until fragrant.

4. Add the veggie broth to the pot, and then whisk in the carrots, potatoes, garbanzo beans, diced tomatoes, lentils, and apricots.

5. Boil on high heat, lower the heat, and then stir in the fresh spinach, simmer the soup, about 30 minutes, or until the veggies and lentils are cooked through and fork-tender.

6. Sprinkle pepper, and salt to taste, cook, 5 more minutes, or until soup becomes thick.

Thai Carrot Soup

Would you want to eat this creamy Thai carrot soup in one sitting? I don't think so! Enriched with lithe coconut milk & coconut curry veggie broth. Yummy!

Preparation Time: 15 minutes

Cooking Time: 15 minutes

Total Time: 30 minutes

Servings: 4

Ingredients:

1/4 cup water

1/2 cup yellow onion chopped

2 tsp. Thai red curry paste add more to taste

2 peeled garlic cloves, chopped

2 tbsp. fresh ginger, peeled, grated

4 large carrots, sliced

2 tbsp. vinegar

3 cups vegetable broth, low sodium

2 7/10 cups light coconut milk

2 tbsp. fresh cilantro, minced

3/8 tbsp. sea salt (if desired)

Directions:

1. Add about 1/4 cup water to a large soup pot, over medium heat, add the yellow onion, sauté, about 3-5 minutes, or until softened.

2. Whisk in the red curry paste, garlic cloves, and fresh ginger, simmer, stirring continuously, about 1 minute more.

3. Add the sliced carrots, vinegar, and vegetable broth, boil, on high heat, and then lower the heat, simmer, covered, between 18 to 20 minutes, or until the carrots are softened. Let stand to cool.

4. Blend 1/2 of the soup in a high powered blender, reduce splatter with the hot fill line guide.

5. Pour back the blended soup into the pot, over low heat, whisk in the light coconut milk, add salt to taste, cook, uncovered until the soup becomes hotter and cooked through.

6. Serve, topped with fresh cilantro or thyme leaves.

Tomato & Yam Soup with Chard

You cannot afford to resist the taste of this delicious soup. Yummy!

Preparation Time: 15 minutes

Cooking Time: 15 minutes

Total Time: 30 minutes

Servings: 4

Ingredients:

1/2 cup water

1/2 large yellow onion, chopped

2 large garlic cloves, minced

1 3/5 cups mushroom, sliced

1/2 large black pepper, chopped

1 large yam, diced

5 cups vegetable broth, low sodium

1/4 tbsp. ground ginger

1/2 tbsp. cayenne pepper

3/4 tbsp. ground coriander

1/2 tsp. sea salt, or to taste

1 1/2 cups tomatoes, chopped

191

1 cup chard, or kale

1 head bok Choy, sliced

2 1/2 tbsp. peanut butter

Directions:

1. Add about 1/2 cup water to the large soup pot, over medium heat, sauté the onions, garlic cloves, and sliced mushrooms, sprinkle black pepper, add the diced yam, simmer, about 6 to 10 minutes, or until the onions are soft.

2. In a mixing bowl, combine about 4 cups of the broth, ground ginger, cayenne pepper, coriander, and salt to taste, thoroughly whisk to combine, and then whisk into the sautéed veggies, simmer, some few more minutes.

3. Add the chard, and bok Choy, stir to combine, and then add the peanut butter plus the remaining vegetable broth to a small bowl, thoroughly whisk until well combined.

4. Pour the mixture into the pot of soup, stir, keep simmering, until cooked through. Let stand to cool, and then serve instantly.

Butternut Squash & Apple Soup

Are you worried about your next weeknight dinner or holiday meal? You would find that answer in this smooth, creamy butternut squash and apple soup! Yummy.

Preparation Time: 25 minutes

Cooking Time: 1 hour, 30 minutes

Total Time: 1 hour, 55 minutes

Servings: 6

Ingredients:

1 1/2 pounds butternut squash, sliced into 2 equal halves, seeds removed

2 apples peeled, seeded, roughly chopped.

3-4 cups low sodium vegetable broth

1/4 cup garlic cloves

1 cup onion, chopped

1 medium chopped celery

3/4 tbsp. cumin, ground

1/4 tbsp. ginger ground

1/4 tbsp. fresh thyme chopped

1/4 tbsp. coriander, dried

1/8 tbsp. dried Ceylon cinnamon

1/4 tsp cayenne pepper, or Tabasco

1/2 tsp. pepper, or to taste

1/2 tsp. sea salt, or to taste

Directions:

1. Preheat the oven to about 400 deg. F.

2. Lightly spray a large baking sheet with cooking oil, and fill with about a 1/4 cup water.

3. Add butternut squash halves to the baking pan, bake, at 400 deg. F, about 45 minutes, or until they become fork tender, let stand to cool, and then remove the flesh, and then set aside. Note: If it's already a cut-up squash directly from the store, line up the baking sheet with a parchment paper, add the pre-cut butternut squash, and then bake for 20 to 25 minutes, or until they are fork-tender.

4. Meanwhile, pour the vegetable broth to a large soup pot, over medium or low heat, sauté the garlic cloves, chopped onions, and celery, add chopped apples, and then baked, cooled butternut squash.

5. In a mixing bowl, add the cumin, ground ginger, thyme, coriander, cinnamon, cayenne pepper or Tabasco, pepper and salt to taste, thoroughly stir to combine or until well incorporated.

6. Pour the spices mixture into the vegetables and squash in the soup pot, simmer, covered, about 40 to 45 minutes, or until the apples are fork-tender, add little water if the soup is thick beyond your satisfaction, let stand to cool.

7. Pour 1/2 of the soup in a blender; slowly blend the soup on low speed, about 3 to 5 minutes, or until crispy and smoothened without lumps.

8. Pour back the blended 1/2 soup into the soup pot, serve instantly into bowls, topped with roasted seeds.

Curried Coconut Lentil potato Soup

This creamy and tasty lentil potato soup is healthy, tasty, delicious, and full of vitamins. Just mix up the Indian spices, cook in your soup pot. Yummy!

Preparation Time: 20 minutes

Cooking Time: 45 minutes

Total Time: 1 hour, 5 minutes

Servings: 6

Ingredients:

1/2 cup water

1 cup onion, chopped

3 minced garlic cloves

4 cups vegetable broth, low sodium

4 cups large sweet potato peeled, cut into 1/4-inch cubes

1 medium red lentils, rinsed

1 cup rinsed cannellini beans, drained

1 1/2 cups tomatoes, crushed

3/4 tbsp. curry powder

1/2 tbsp. dried cumin

1/8 tbsp. Ceylon cinnamon

2 tsp. ginger, minced

1/2 tbsp. garam masala

1 1/2 tbsp. maple syrup

1 1/3 cups evaporated milk

1 1/2 tsp coconut extract

2/3 cup water

1/5 cup peanut butter

1/2 tsp. pepper, or to taste

1/2 tsp. sea salt, or to taste

Directions:

1. Add a little amount of water to a large pot, over medium heat, sauté the onion, garlic cloves, about 3-4 minutes, or until softened and fragrant.

2. Pour in the vegetable broth, add the potato, lentils, cannellini beans, and crushed tomatoes.

3. In a large mixing bowl, add the curry powder, cumin, cinnamon, ginger, and garam masala, thoroughly stir to combine, top with 1 and 1/2 tablespoons of maple syrup.

4. In a separate bowl, add the evaporated milk, coconut extract, and water, thoroughly stir to combine, pour milk mixture into the spices mixture, thoroughly stir to combine, stir in the peanut butter, stir well, about 2 minutes, or until well incorporated.

5. Pour in the mixtures into the soup pot, sprinkle pepper and salt to tastes, simmer, covered, about 45 minutes to an hour, or until well cooked. Let stand to cool.

6. Pour half of the soup to a blender; blend slowly until smoothened and crispy.

7. Pour the blended half soup back into the pot, serve instantly, topped with flaxseeds, chia seeds, or any of your favorite seeds.

Roasted Tomato Pepper Bisque

You would derive a satisfactory flavor in this soup without the use of any cream after roasting these tomatoes and vegetables. Yummy!

Preparation Time: 15 minutes

Cooking Time: 20 minutes

Total Time: 35 minutes

Servings: 4

Ingredients:

5 large tomatoes, quartered

3 large leeks, or 2 large yellow onions

1/2 cup black pepper, seeded, quartered

1/2 tsp. pepper, or to taste

1/2 tsp. salt, or to taste

4 garlic cloves, peeled

2 1/2 cups vegetable broth, low sodium

1/2 cup plain yogurt

1/4 tbsp. paprika

Directions:

1. Preheat the oven to about 400 deg. F.

2. Line up a baking pan with a tin foil or parchment paper.

3. Add the quartered tomatoes, leeks or yellow onions, black pepper to the baking pan, sprinkle pepper, and salt.

4. Bake, at 400 deg. F., about 5 minutes, add the peeled garlic cloves, keep roasting the veggies, about 15 minutes, or until they are browned and fork-tender and fragrant, ensure stirring halfway through.

5. Transfer the roasted vegetables into a large pot, pour in the 2 and 1/2 cups vegetable broth, sauté, a few more minutes, let stand to cool.

6. Process half of the soup with a high powered blender, until smoothened and crispy, and then pour the blended soup back into the soup pot, simmer until heated through.

7. Whisk in the plain yogurt, taste to see if more would be needed, serve, topped with paprika.

Creamy Potato and Spinach Soup

Serve this creamy, rich, fat-free, creamy potato and kale soup with toasted whole-grain bread. Enjoy with your family! Yummy!

Preparation Time: 15 minutes

Cooking Time: 20 minutes

Total Time: 35 minutes

Servings: 4

Ingredients:

4 cups vegetable broth, low sodium

1/2 cup onion, diced

1 garlic clove, chopped fine

1 large carrot, diced

1 rib celery, diced

1 cup potatoes, diced

1 cup parsley, finely chopped

1/2 tbsp. black pepper, fresh ground

1/2 tbsp. salt (if desired)

1 tsp chia seeds (if desired)

3 large spinach leaves, sliced into thin ribbons

4 cups of rice milk, unsweetened

2/5 cups flour, or 4 tsp. cornstarch

1 1/4 cups yeast, nutritional

Directions:

1. Add the vegetable broth to a large soup pot, over medium heat, sauté the onion and garlic, about 2-3 minutes, or until softened and translucent.

2. Add the diced carrots, celery, potatoes, 1/2 cup parsley, black pepper, salt (if using), chia seeds, and spinach leaves, bring to a boil, about 13 to 15 minutes, or until tender.

3. In a mixing bowl, add flour or cornstarch with about 3/4 cup water, thoroughly stir to combine.

4. Meanwhile, boil the rice milk in a saucepot, over medium heat, about 1-2 minutes, pour the liquefied flour mixture into the boiling rice milk, stir thoroughly until thickened, turn off the heat, add yeast.

5. Turn off the heat from the soup, and then add the milk sauce, and the remaining 1/2 cup parsley. Stir to combine, serve instantly.

Vegetable Soup with Ravioli

Are you looking for a perfect, easy, and daily dinner? This Italian flavorful veggie soup with ravioli is okay for you, your kids, entire family, loved ones, and guests. Yummy!

Preparation Time: 30 minutes

Cooking Time: 20 minutes

Total Time: 50 minutes

Servings: 6

Ingredients:

2 medium chopped bell peppers (about 1 cup)

1 cup diced carrots, peeled

1 cup onion, diced

1/8 tbsp red pepper or to taste, crushed (if desired)

2 garlic cloves, minced

1 3/4 cups crushed tomatoes, fire-roasted

5 cups vegetable broth, low sodium

1/2 tbsp. marjoram, or 1/2 tbsp. dried basil

1 cup garbanzo beans

2 cups diced zucchini

5-6 spinach leaves, roughly chopped

1/2 tsp. pepper, or to taste

1/2 tsp. sea salt, or to taste

2 cups of water

1/2 pound ravioli, fresh or frozen

Directions:

1. Add 1/5 cup water to a large soup pot, add the bell peppers, carrots, and onions, simmer, over medium heat, about 3-4 minutes.

2. Add crushed red pepper and garlic cloves, simmer 1 more minute.

3. Add the crushed tomatoes, vegetable broth, marjoram, garbanzo beans, zucchini, and spinach leaves, bring to a boil over medium heat.

4. Sprinkle pepper and salt to taste.

5. Add about 2 cups water to a boiling pot, sauté the ravioli over medium or low heat, cook based on the directions on the ravioli package.

6. Add the cooked ravioli to the soup pot, let stand to cool, and then serve instantly.

Creamy Curried Cauliflower Soup

This cauliflower soup is no doubt, one of my favorite soups. It's very easy to prepare, and you will want to request more. Enjoy with guests!

Preparation Time: 20 minutes

Cooking Time: 45 minutes

Total Time: 1 hour, 5 minutes

Servings: 5

Ingredients:

1/2 pound potatoes peeled, cut into 1 1/2" pieces

1/2 pound yams peeled and cut, into 1 1/2" pieces

1 1/2 medium red bell pepper, coarsely chopped,

1 large head of cauliflower, cut into about 1 1/2" pieces

1 1/2 cups rinsed kidney beans, drained

3 medium carrots, sliced

1 medium onion, diced

1 1/2 tbsp. red curry paste

1/8 tsp. red pepper, crushed

1 tbsp. fresh, grated ginger

1/4 tbsp. sea salt, or to taste

4 cups vegetable broth, low sodium

1 14 oz can light canned coconut milk

Directions:

1. In a large soup pot, over medium or low heat, combine the potatoes, yams, red bell pepper, cauliflower, kidney beans, sliced carrots, and diced onion.

2. Add the red curry paste, crushed red pepper, ginger, and salt to taste to the sautéed veggies in the soup pot.

3. Pour in the vegetable broth, simmer, covered, on low, about 40 to 45 minutes, or until the vegetables are fork-tender.

4. Whisk in the coconut milk, keep heating until heated through.

5. Let stand to cool, serve instantly.

Gazpacho & Cucumber Smoothie

The process is very simple. Just puree in a blender or food processor and that's all. Nourishing and delicious!

Preparation Time: 10 minutes

Total Time: 10 minutes

Servings: 4

Ingredients:

1 1/2 cups apple juice

1 1/2 cups tomato juice

1 medium cucumber, roughly chopped

1 medium red onion roughly, chopped

1 green pepper, roughly chopped

1/4 tbsp. hot sauce

1/4 tbsp. salt, or to taste

1/4 tbsp. pepper, or to taste

Directions:

Add all the ingredients to a high powered blender, slowly blend, and later increase the speed to 5, blend, about 1 to 2 minutes, chill in the fridge.

Papaya Gazpacho & Avocado

This meal contains tropical fruits like papaya and avocado mixed with tomato and lemon juice. Flavorful, tasty, and delicious. Yummy!

Preparation Time: 20 minutes

Total Time: 10 minutes

Servings: 4

Ingredients:

1 1/2 cups tomato juice

1 1/2 cups vinegar

1 ripe, peeled papaya, seeded and diced

1 red bell pepper (or any color bell pepper) seeded and diced

1 medium yellow onion, diced

1 diced avocado, cut into 1/4

1/4 cup fresh lemon juice

1 tbsp. cayenne pepper

1/2 medium cilantro, finely chopped

1/2 tsp. salt, or to taste (if desired)

1/2 tsp. ground pepper, or to taste (if desired)

Direction:

Add all the ingredients to a large mixing bowl, stir to combine, blend in a high powered blender, place in the fridge for a couple of hours, serve chilled.

Cold Cucumber Soup

Topped and flavored with avocado and fresh mint. You could serve this cold cucumber soup for a refreshing lunch in the hot summer.

Preparation Time: 15 minutes

Total Time: 10 minutes

Servings: 6

Ingredients:

1/2-3/4 cup water

5 3/5 cups cucumber peeled, seeded and cut into 1/3 pieces

8 large spinach leaves, roughly chopped

1 minced garlic clove, skinned

1/2 medium yellow onion, roughly chopped

1/2 tbsp. maple syrup

3/4 cup plain yogurt

2 tbsp. white wine

1 chopped avocado

1/2 tsp. salt, or to taste (if desired)

Directions:

1. Add about a 1/2-3/4 cup water to a food processor, add cucumber, spinach leaves, garlic clove, onion, maple syrup, yogurt, and white wine, and process about, 4 to 5 minutes, or until smoothened.

2. Pour the pureed mixture into a bowl, place in the fridge, about 2 hours, or until well chilled.

3. Serve the chilled soup into bowls, top with the chopped avocado.

Hearty Vegetable Soup

You will find this one-pot meal tasty, enriched with fruits and proteins.

Preparation Time: 20 minutes

Cooking Time: 30 minutes

Total Time: 50 minutes

Servings: 6

Ingredients:

1 medium red lentils

5 cups vegetable broth, low sodium

1/2 head cauliflower florets bite-sized

3 garlic cloves, minced

1 large, chopped onion

2 medium carrots, sliced 1/2 inch thick

1 cup red bell peppers, coarsely chopped

1 1/2 cups tomatoes, diced

6 large parsley leaves

1 1/2 cups unsweetened pumpkin puree

1 1/2 cups rinsed kidney beans, drained

Directions:

1. In a large soup pot, add the vegetable broth, sauté over medium heat,

add the lentils, simmer, about 3-5 minutes.

2. Add the cauliflower florets, garlic cloves, onion, carrots, red bell

peppers, tomatoes, and parsley.

3. Simmer, covered, about 30 minutes, or until the veggies are tender, add some water to thin if required.

4. Stir in the kidney beans pumpkin puree until well incorporated, thoroughly cook until well heated, let stand to cool, serve, topped with a large green salad.

Lentil Pea Soup

This lentil pea soup is enriched with veggies and low-fat coconut milk. With this, you cannot feel cozy on the inside.

Preparation Time: 15 minutes

Cooking Time: 45 minutes

Total Time: 1 hour

Servings: 8

Ingredients:

2 1/2 tbsp. water

1 medium celery, chopped

2 medium carrot, chopped

1 onion chopped, large

6 garlic cloves, finely chopped

3/4 tbsp. turmeric, ground

1 tbsp. coriander, ground

1 tbsp. cumin, ground

8 cups vegetable broth, low sodium

1 1/2 cups split peas

1 1/2 cups green lentils

1 1/2 cups orange lentils

1/4 cup vinegar

1 cup light canned coconut milk

1/2 tsp. salt, or to taste

1/2 tsp. pepper, or to taste

Directions:

1. Fill a large pot with about 1/4 cup water, sauté the celery, carrots, and onions over medium or low heat, about 4-5 minutes, or until tender.

2. In a mixing bowl, add the garlic cloves, turmeric, coriander, and cumin, thoroughly whisk to combine.

3. Stir in the garlic-spices mixture, and then stir in the vegetable broth, simmer at high heat.

4. Add the split peas, green and orange lentils, lower the heat, simmer, covered, about 40-45 minutes.

5. Stir in the coconut milk, vinegar, and then sprinkle salt, and pepper to taste.

6. Serve, topped with fresh plain yogurt.

5. Stir in the coconut milk

Mushroom Brown Rice Soup

This creamy soup is healthy, tasty, nourishing, and full of vitamins. Yummy!

Preparation Time: 20 minutes

Cooking Time: 20 minutes

Total Time: 40 minutes

Servings: 4

Ingredients:

1/4 cup water

1/2 yellow onion, chopped

2 garlic cloves, minced

8 ounces of mushrooms sliced.

4 cups vegetable broth, low sodium

1 small zucchini, sliced

1/2 cup brown rice, uncooked

1/2 tbsp. dried oregano

1/4 tbsp. thyme

2 tbsp. flour

1 cup plain yogurt

1/2 tsp. sea salt, or to taste

1/2 tsp. Pepper to taste

Directions:

1. Add the 1/4 cup water to a large soup pot, sauté the onions, about 2-3 minutes, or until translucent.

2. Add the garlic cloves, mushrooms, simmer, until the mushrooms begin

wilting.

3. Stir in the vegetable broth, add the zucchini, brown rice, oregano, and thyme, simmer until the mushrooms are cooked through.

4. In a small mixing bowl, add 1/2 cup plain yogurt, flour, thoroughly stir to combine, whisk into the mushroom mixture, and then add the remaining yogurt.

5. Whisk until well incorporated, simmer until creamy and thickened. Sprinkle salt and pepper to taste.

Tomato Coconut Curry Soup

This soup contains a sufficient amount of root vegetables that are classic for warming your body. Yummy!

Preparation Time: 20 minutes

Cooking Time: 60 minutes

Total Time: 1 hour, 20 minutes

Servings: 6

Ingredients:

1/4 cup water

1 cup onion, finely chopped

1 rib celery, finely chopped

1/4 tbsp. curry powder

1/8 tbsp. ground coriander

2 potatoes peeled and diced

1 carrot peeled and finely chopped

1 1/2 cups stewed tomatoes, or diced

2 cups vegetable broth, low sodium

1/2 cup coconut milk

sea salt and pepper to taste

1/3 cup nutritional yeast (if desired)

2 pinches hot sauce

Chopped parsley for garnish

Directions:

1. In a large pot, heat a 1/4 cup water over medium or low heat, add the onion and celery, simmer, about 10 to 15 minutes, or until tender.

2. In a mixing bowl, add the coriander, and curry powder, stir into the sautéed veggies.

3. Add the potatoes, carrots, simmer, about 10 minutes more, add the stewed or diced tomatoes, vegetable broth, bring to a boil at high heat.

4. Reduce the heat, simmer, covered, 30 to 35 minutes, or until the potatoes are softened. Let stand to cool.

5. After being cooled, blend half of the soup in a high powered blender, blend until crispy and smoothened without lumps, and then pour back into the soup pot, thoroughly whisk to combine.

6. Add the coconut milk; keep simmering, about 5 minutes, sprinkle pepper and salt to taste, add yeast (if using), and hot sauce, stir to combine

7. Serve, topped with fresh parsley.

Chickpea Salad Sandwich

This chicken salad recipe is very rich in fiber and protein. Serve with tomato, avocado, and sprouts. You will love the taste. Yummy!

Preparation Time: 15 minutes

Total Time: 15 minutes

Servings: 4

Ingredients:

1 1/2 cups rinsed chickpeas, drained

1/4 cup sweet pickle, chopped

1/2 medium red onion, minced

2 celery stalks, finely chopped

217

3 tbsp. sour cream

2 tsp. yellow mustard

1/4 tsp. ground black pepper, or to taste

1/4 tsp. sea salt, or to taste

Directions:

1. Add the chickpeas to a large bowl, and then mash with a fork or a potato masher.

2. Stir in the sweet pickle, red onion, celery stalks, sour cream, and yellow mustard.

3. Sprinkle black pepper and salt to taste. Serve.

Sloppy Joes

This is a quick, easy recipe prepared with crumbled tempeh, and garnished with mustard. Yummy!

Preparation Time: 20 minutes

Cooking Time: 20 minutes

Total Time: 40 minutes

Servings: 5

Ingredients:

16 oz. tempeh original soy, crumbled

2 garlic cloves, minced

1 small yellow onion, chopped

1 red bell pepper, chopped

16 oz tomato ketchup

3 tbsp. yellow mustard

2/5 cup red wine vinegar, apple cider vinegar

4 tsp. Vegan Worcestershire sauce

1/2 tsp. sea salt, or to taste

1/2 tsp. pepper, or to taste

Directions:

1. In a large sauté pan, add a little water, sauté the onion, garlic cloves, and red bell pepper, about 2-3 minutes, or until wilted.

2. Add the crumbled tempeh, tomato ketchup, Worcestershire sauce, yellow mustard, red wine vinegar, pepper, and salt to taste.

3. Simmer, covered, about 15 to 18 minutes, or until flavorful. Serve.

Spicy Falafel Burger

This falafel burger is delicious, tasty, and flavorful. Top with lettuce, pickles, tomatoes, and creamy tahini dressing.

Preparation Time: 15 minutes

Cooking Time: 20 minutes

Total Time: 35 minutes

Servings: 4

Ingredients:

1 1/2 cups cannellini beans chickpeas

2 smashed garlic cloves

1 small onion, chopped

1/4 tbsp. coriander

1/2 medium parsley, chopped

1/3 tsp. baking soda

1/4 tbsp. cumin

2 1/2 tbsp. chopped mint

1/8 tbsp. hot sauce

1 tbsp. white wine

1/2 tsp sea salt, or to taste

Chickpea flour

4 whole wheat burger buns

Sliced tomatoes

Red onion, lettuce and tahini dressing for serving

Tahini Dressing:

1/4 cup tahini

juice of 1 lemon

sea salt to taste

Directions:

1. Preheat the oven to about 400 deg. F.

2. Add half of the cannellini beans in a blender or food processor, pulse, until well chopped but does not have to be smooth.

3. Transfer the processed beans into a large bowl.

4. Pulse the remaining cannellini beans along with the garlic, onion, coriander, parsley, baking soda, cumin, mint, hot sauce, white wine, and salt to taste.

5. Blend until thickened, stir in the chickpea flour, shape into balls.

6. Apply a cooking spray on the baking sheet, place the shaped balls on the baking sheet, bake, at 400 deg. F., about 16-20 minutes, flipping halfway through, until firm and golden.

7. Serve, topped with a dollop of the tahini dressing.

Tempeh Reuben Sandwich

Get your health boosted with this version of a sandwich. As satisfying as your favorite. Yummy!

Preparation Time: 15 minutes

Total Time: 15 minutes

Servings: 4

Ingredients:

1 tbsp. prepared yellow mustard

1 tbsp. sour cream

2 slices whole-grain bread, toasted

2 pickle slices

Half package tempeh, cut to bread size

2/3 medium sauerkraut

Directions:

1. Rub the yellow mustard and sour cream to the toasted bread slices, and then serve, topped with slices of pickles, tempeh, and sauerkraut.

Curried Tempeh Lettuce Wraps

Enjoy this easy curried tempeh lettuce wraps with a touch of mango chutney. Healthy, Tasty, & Delicious!

Preparation Time: 15 minutes

Total Time: 15 minutes

Servings: 3

Ingredients:

8 ounces tempeh, original soy crumbled

1 cup diced apple

2/3 medium raisins

2 1/2 tbsp. walnuts

1 celery stalk, diced

1/2 diced cucumber

1/2 medium mango chutney

1/2 tbsp red pepper flakes

1/2 medium red onion, diced

2 tbsp. sour cream

1/5 cup vinegar

1/2 tsp. sea salt, or to taste

1/2 tsp. pepper, or to taste

Directions:

1. In a large mixing bowl, add all the ingredients, thoroughly whisk to combine.

2. Serve, wrapped in a lettuce leaf, and topped with sprouts though optional.

Tofu Eggless Salad Sandwich

In just 5 minutes, you're done preparing this delicious Tofu Eggless Salad Sandwich. Yummy!

Preparation Time: 15 minutes

Total Time: 15 minutes

Servings: 3

Ingredients:

1 block firm organic tofu drained and pressed

225

2/3 medium chopped celery

1/2 medium chopped red onion

2 sweet pickles

1/5 cup yellow mustard, prepared

2 tbsp. sour cream, or mayonnaise

1/2 medium chopped parsley

1/4 tbsp. curry powder

1/2 tsp. pepper, or to taste

1/2 tsp. sea salt, or to taste

8 pieces low oil sourdough bread

Topping:

tomato slices

sprouts

1 medium sliced avocado (if desired)

Directions:

1. In a large bowl, add the tofu, break into smaller pieces using a fork.

2. In another bowl, add the celery, red onion, sweet pickles, yellow mustard, sour cream, parsley, curry powder, pepper, and salt, thoroughly stir to combine.

3. Pour mixture into tofu pieces, whisk to combine until well incorporated.

4. Serve, topped with tomato slices, sprouts, and avocado (if desired)

Grilled Mushroom, Eggplant Sandwich

Top this flavorful recipe with tomato and basil slices. You would love the taste and not want to enjoy alone. Yummy!

Preparation Time: 25 minutes

Cooking Time: 10 minute

Total Time: 35 minutes

Servings: 4

Ingredients:

8 slices whole-grain bread

3-4 large portobello mushrooms cut in 1/2 slices

2 medium eggplants cut into 1/2 slices

3 garlic cloves minced

1/2 cup lemon juice

6-7 basil leaves chopped (optional)

2 1/2 tbsp. mayonnaise

Directions:

1. Add the Portobello mushrooms and eggplants to a large baking pan,

2. Add, and cover all the sides with the garlic cloves and lemon juice, and then, marinate, about 25 to 30 minutes, or more.

3. Line up a baking sheet with a tin foil or parchment paper, preheat an oven to about 350 deg. F., in a single layer, broil the vegetables, about 5 to 6 minutes, flip, broil 5 to 6 minutes.

4. Top with the basil leaves (if using), and for a sandwich, top mushrooms and eggplants on grain bread with mayonnaise, add onions, avocado, tomato, and lettuce.

Vegetable Sandwich

The use of roasted red peppers makes this yummy veggie sandwich spicy. Enjoy with guests.

Preparation Time: 15 minutes

Cooking Time: 10 minute

Total Time: 25 minutes

Servings: 2

Ingredients:

1/2 cup zucchini, sliced 1/4" lengthwise

3/4 cup water

1/4 tbsp. Worcestershire sauce

4 whole-grain bread, slices

2 tbsp. yellow mustard (if desired)

2 large jarred red peppers, roasted

2 red onion, sliced

3/5 cup hummus

2 leaves romaine lettuce

Directions:

1. In large sauté pan, over medium heat, add water and Worcestershire sauce.

2. Add the zucchini slices, simmer, covered, about 3-5 minutes, or until wilted.

3. Gently toast the bread slices, toss each side with the yellow mustard (if using).

4. Spread the onion slices, roasted red peppers, and hummus on the zucchini, and then top with romaine lettuce, enjoy.

Black Bean Mushroom Burger

Enjoy this black beans and mushroom burger over and over again with your guests and loved ones.

Preparation Time: 15 minutes

Cooking Time: 10 minute

Total Time: 25 minutes

Servings: 4

Ingredients:

1/4 cup water

1 cup onions, diced

1/4 tbsp. dried cumin

1 garlic clove minced

1/2 pound mushrooms, roughly chopped

1 medium red wine

3 1/3 tbsp. soy sauce

3 slices ole grain bread lightly toasted

1/4 cup sun-dried tomatoes, soaked in 1/2 cup hot water

1 1/2 cups black beans rinsed and drained, low sodium

1/2 tsp. pepper, or to taste

1/2 tsp. sea salt, or to taste

Directions:

1. Preheat the oven to about 375 deg. F.

2. Add 1/4 cup water to a large skillet, sauté over medium-high heat.

3. Add the diced onions, sauté, about 3-4 minutes, or until tender and translucent.

4. Whisk in the dried cumin, garlic clove, and mushrooms, simmer, covered, about 4-6 minutes, or until the mushrooms become fragrant.

5. Add the soy sauce and red wine, simmer, until the cooking liquid evaporates or reduces to half, and then remove from heat, let stand to cool slightly.

6. Add the toasted bread slices to a food processor, and then process, to break into bread crumbs.

7. Pour the bread crumbs into a small bowl, and then add the black beans, sun-dried tomatoes, and mushroom mixture to the food processor.

8. Pulse until mixed, but does not have to be smooth, transfer the processed mixture into a bowl, add the bread crumbs into the mixture, sprinkle pepper, and salt to taste.

9. Thoroughly whisk to combine, divide into 4 portions, and shape into about 4 thick burger patties.

10. Place directly on a baking sheet coated with cooking spray, bake, at 375 deg. F., 5 minutes on each side, flip n order to brown on the other side, 5 minutes more. Enjoy.

Vegan Yogurt Parfait with Berries & Granola

Spice up your day with this delicious, healthy, and nutritious plant-based breakfast.

Preparation Time: 5 minutes

Total Time: 5 minutes

Servings: 2

Ingredients:

1 cup plain yogurt

1 1/2 medium frozen berries, defrosted

2/3 medium homemade granola

233

1/2 tbsp. maple syrup (if desired)

2 tsp. farro

Directions:

1. Add one-third of the whole fruit to the bottom of a glass container.

2. Add a quarter cup of the plain yogurt on the fruit, add about a 1/2 tablespoon maple syrup if desired.

3. Add 1/3 medium of granola directly on the fruit in the container

3. Top with the remaining granola, sprinkle the farro on top and then repeat the fruit, plain yogurt, and granola layers.

Chai Spice Apple Muffins

These muffins are very easy to prepare, the combination of applesauce and whole grains make it lovely. Yummy!

Preparation Time: 20 minutes

Cooking Time: 30 minutes

Total Time: 50 minutes

Servings: 12

Ingredients:

1/2 ounce ground flax seed

2/5 cup water

5 tbsp. oats

1/2 tbsp. baking soda

3 medium whole wheat flour

1 tbsp. chai spice mix

1/8 tbsp. salt (if desired)

1/2 cup mashed banana

1/2 tbsp. non-alcoholic vanilla extract

2 and 1/2 tbsp. non-dairy milk

5 ounces applesauce

1/2 medium maple syrup (if desired)

1/3 cup walnuts

1/4 tbsp. cinnamon, dried

1/4 tbsp. ginger, dried

1/4 tbsp. cardamom, dried

1/4 tbsp. nutmeg, dried

Chai Spice Mix

1/2 cup peeled & cored apples, chopped

Directions:

1. In a small bowl, mix flaxseed with water, place aside to thicken.

2. Preheat an oven to about 350 deg. F., lightly spray a non-stick muffin tray with oil.

3. Thoroughly whisk the dry ingredients together in a small or medium-sized mixing bowl. Of course, the dry ingredients are oats, baking soda, whole wheat flour, chai spice mix, and salt (if using).

4. Add the mashed banana, vanilla extract, milk, apple sauce, and maple syrup (if using) to a separate bowl, thoroughly whisk to combine.

5. Add walnuts, cinnamon, ginger, cardamom, nutmeg, and spice mix into the wet mixture, thoroughly whisk to combine.

5. Add a dollop of mixture into each tin, and then sprinkle the chopped apples.

6. Bake, at about 350 deg. F., about 20 to 30 minutes, or until a toothpick inserted into a muffin tin comes out clean.

Heart Healthy Chocolate Hummus

Enjoy this chocolaty and creamy treat without your waistline getting affected. Yummy!

Preparation Time: 10 minutes

Total Time: 10 minutes

Servings: 6

Ingredients:

1 1/2 cups rinsed chickpeas, drained, no salt added

2 1/2 tbsp. chocolate, unsweetened

1/4 cup corn syrup

1/2 tbsp. almond or vanilla extract

2/5 cup plain yogurt

1/5 cup tahini (if desired)

1/4 tsp sea salt (if desired)

Directions:

1. Add the rinsed, drained chickpeas to a blender.

2. Add the unsweetened chocolate, corn syrup, almond or vanilla extract

237

(the non-alcoholic type), tahini (if using), plain yogurt, and then sprinkle salt (if using).

3. Blend, a few seconds, scrape both sides down with a spatula.

4. Add a more plain yogurt until the desired consistency is reached for dipping fruit.

5. Serve, topped with pineapple juice, strawberries.

Spicy Roasted Red Pepper Dip

You could pound on this creamy zesty dip combined with hummus and nuts. Tasty, nourishing, and delicious.

Preparation Time: 10 minutes

Total Time: 10 minutes

Servings: 6

Ingredients:

5 oz. roasted red peppers, rinsed and drained

1 medium chopped hazelnuts

2 whole-grain bread slices

2 garlic cloves, roughly chopped

2 tsp. balsamic vinegar

1/4 tbsp. cumin, ground

1/8 tbsp. red pepper flakes

1/4 tbsp. sea salt, or to taste

Directions:

1. Add the roasted red peppers, hazelnuts, bread slices, garlic cloves, vinegar, cumin, red pepper flakes, and salt to the blender or food processor.

2. Pulse, a few minutes, or until creamy and smoothened.

3. Transfer the mixture onto a serving bowl, and then top with celery, and carrots, or any of your favorite sliced raw vegetables.

Chia Oats & Berries Snack

This chia oats snack is very tasty, and it's easily prepared. Enjoy when combined with nuts and fruits. Yummy!

Preparation Time: 10 minutes

Total Time: 10 minutes

Servings: 1

Ingredients:

1/2 medium rolled oats

1/2 cups plain yogurt

1/8 tbsp. Ceylon cinnamon

1/8 tbsp. vanilla extract, non-alcoholic preferred

1/5 cup flax seeds

1/4 tsp. liquid stevia, or 1 tsp. maple syrup

Topping:

2 1/2 tbsp. fresh raspberries, or frozen

2 1/2 tbsp. fresh cranberries, or frozen

1/2 oz. hazelnuts, or walnuts

Directions:

1. Add rolled oats, cinnamon, yogurt, non-alcoholic type of vanilla or almond extract, flax seeds, and the sweetener of your choice (liquid stevia or maple syrup).

2. Thoroughly whisk to combine, Place in the fridge all through the night.

3. Serve, topped with berries and nuts in the morning.

Trail Mix, Nuts With Berries

Enjoy these healthy fats and low sugar trail mix in the morning. Yummy!

Preparation Time: 10 minutes

Total Time: 10 minutes

Servings: 12

Ingredients:

1/2 cup soybeans, dry-roasted

1/2 medium walnuts

1/2 cup chia seeds

1/4 cup almonds

1 medium freeze-dried berries (blueberries, strawberries, cherries)

Dark Chocolate Oat Clusters

1 medium whole oats

1/4 cup unsweetened chocolate chips

Directions:

1. Add the soybeans, walnuts, chia seeds, almonds, and berries to a mixing bowl.

2. Whisk in the oats, and melt in the chocolate, stir to combine, and then place in the fridge overnight. Serve in the morning.

Oil-Free Potato, Yam or Tortilla Chips

You could serve a snack with dips and salsas even at parties all through the year. Make use of any of your favorite natural seasonings. Yummy!

Preparation Time: 15 minutes

Cooking Time: 8 minutes

Total Time: 23 minutes

Servings: 4

Ingredients:

2-3 large dry Potatoes or Yams sliced thinly by hand or with a mandolin

12, 6" corn tortillas

1/2 tsp. salt, or to taste

Directions:

1. Preheat the oven to about 400 deg. F.

2. Line up a baking sheet with a tin foil or parchment paper.

3. Sprinkle about 1/4 cup water on the corn tortillas if too dry.

4. Lightly sprinkle salt to taste.

5. Bake, at 400 deg. F., about 8-10 minutes, flip over, bake, 8-10 more minutes, but be watchful to prevent burning. Let stand to cool, serve.

Banana Bread with Maple Glaze

What a delicious and healthy treat with banana bread topped with maple glaze. Your loved ones and guests will love it. Yummy!

Preparation Time: 30 minutes

Cooking Time: 25 minutes

Total Time: 55 minutes

Servings: 10

Ingredients:

7/10 cup almond milk, unsweetened

1 tsp lemon juice

1 1/2 oz. buttermilk

1 medium banana, mashed

1/4 cup maple syrup or 1 tbsp. liquid stevia

1 1/2 tbsp vanilla extract, non-alcoholic

1/4 tbsp. sea salt

3/4 cup cornstarch

1/4 tbsp. cinnamon, dried

1 medium rolled oats

3/4 tbsp. baking powder

1/4 tbsp. baking soda

1/2 cup unsweetened chocolate chips

1/4 cup chopped hazelnuts (if desired)

1/5 cup maple syrup (if desired)

1/4 tbsp. cinnamon, ground (if desired)

Directions:

1. Preheat the oven to about 350 deg. F.

2. Add the almond milk and lemon juice to a large mixing bowl, thoroughly whisk to combine, and then set aside about 5 minutes.

3. In another large bowl, add the buttermilk, mashed banana, maple syrup, vanilla extract, and salt to taste.

4. Stir thoroughly the cornstarch, cinnamon, oats, baking powder, and soda in a separate bowl.

5. Transfer the almond milk mixture into the maple syrup mixture, thoroughly whisk to combine, until well incorporated.

6. Whisk in the milk mixture into the cornstarch mixture, thoroughly whisk to combine.

7. Stir in the hazelnuts (if using) and unsweetened chocolate chips.

8. Line up a baking pan with a tin foil or parchment paper or spray with cooking oil, and then pour the mixture onto the pan, leaving spaces.

9. Bake, at 350 deg. F., about 25 minutes, or until a toothpick could come out clean when inserted.

10. Let stand to cool, and then serve, topped with a mixture of dried cinnamon and maple syrup if desired.

Carrot Chocolate Chip Cookies
You can't afford to miss the taste. Yummy!

Preparation Time: 20 minutes

Cooking Time: 50 minutes

Total Time: 1 hr, 10 minutes

Servings: 30

Ingredients:

1/2 cup dry quinoa, dry

2/3 cup water

3 tbsp. ground chia seeds

1/2 cup water

1 cup old fashioned oats

1 cup cornstarch

1/2 tbsp. baking powder

1/2 tbsp. baking soda

1/2 tsp. Ceylon cinnamon

3/4 tsp. sea salt, or to taste

1 medium coconut sugar

1 cup carrots, finely grated

1/2 cup buttermilk

1/2 cup applesauce, unsweetened

1/2 cup ripe banana, mashed

1/2 tbsp. vanilla extract, non-alcoholic

1 medium unsweetened chocolate chips (if desired)

1/2 cup hazelnuts

Directions:

1. Preheat the oven to about 350 deg. F.

2. Spray a baking sheet with cooking oil, or line up using a parchment paper.

3. Add the chia seeds and water to a bowl, mix, and let sit, some few minutes.

4. Add 2/3 cup water to a sauté pan, over medium heat, add the quinoa, simmer, about 10-15 minutes, let stand to cool.

5. Meanwhile, add the oats, cornstarch, cooked and cooled quinoa, baking powder, baking soda, cinnamon, and salt to a separate bowl, thoroughly whisk to combine.

6. In a separate bowl, mix up the coconut sugar, carrots, buttermilk, applesauce, mashed banana, vanilla extract, chocolate chips, and hazelnuts, thoroughly whisk to mix.

7. Pour in the cornstarch mixture into the applesauce mixture, stir thoroughly to mix.

8. Spread a dollop of large spoonfuls onto the baking sheet, bake, about 20-25 minutes, with frequent checking to prevent burning. Let stand to cool, and then enjoy.

Heart Healthy Smoothie

You can drink this smoothie at any time of the day. Tasty!

Preparation Time: 5 minutes

Total Time: 5 minutes

Servings: 1

Ingredients:

1 2/3 ounces organic blueberries, frozen

1 2/3 ounces organic strawberries, frozen

1 2/3 organic cranberries, frozen

3 large leaves romaine lettuce

2 1/2 tbsp. oats, old fashioned

2 tsp. flaxseeds, ground

7 1/2 tbsp. soy milk, unsweetened

2 1/2 tbsp. pomegranate juice

2 tsp. peanut butter

1/2 cup water (if desired)

Directions:

1. Add all the berries (blueberries, cranberries, and strawberries) to a blender.

2. Top with romaine lettuce, oats, flaxseeds, soy milk, juice, butter, puree until smoothened and without lumps.

3. Add more water if too thick, serve instantly.

Turmeric-Apple Smoothie

You could always have all the ingredients to prepare this turmeric-apple smoothie. Serve as tasty refreshment at any time of the day!

Preparation Time: 5 minutes

Total Time: 5 minutes

Servings: 2

Ingredients:

2 cups of soy milk

5 ounces bananas, frozen, broken into pieces

1/2 tbsp. dried and peeled turmeric, grated

2 tsp. chia seeds

1 cup apple, frozen

1/8 tbsp cinnamon, dried

1/8 tbsp. vanilla extract, non-alcoholic

1/2 tbsp. fresh ginger, peeled, grated

1/2 tsp. pepper, dried

Directions:

1. In a blender, add milk, bananas, turmeric, chia seeds, apple, cinnamon, ginger, vanilla extract, and pepper, blend until smoothened and without lumps.

2. Scrape all the sides as necessary, serve instantly.

Muesli With Nuts & Raisins

Thinking about nuts, seeds, and grains that are oil-free for a vegan meal? Muesli just got okay for you! Yummy!

Preparation Time: 20 minutes

Total Time: 20 minutes

Servings: 8

Ingredients:

10 ounces oats, old fashioned

2 ounces of wheat flakes

1 medium hemp hearts

1 cup quinoa Flakes

5 tbsp. ground flaxseeds

2 and 1/2 ounces pumpkin seeds, raw

1 medium almond, slivered

1 medium coconut flakes

1 medium walnut

1/8 pound raisins

1/2 tbsp. Ceylon cinnamon

1/2 tbsp. almond extract

Directions:

1. Add all ingredients to a large bowl, Whisk thoroughly to mix.

2. Transfer onto a glass jar, cover with the lid

3. Serve, topped with berries and almond milk.

Banana Bread Spicy Mix

You would love the way this banana bread spicy mix is being prepared. Easy, healthy, tasty, and delicious! Yummy!

Preparation Time: 30 minutes

Cooking Time: 25 minutes

Total Time: 55 minutes

Servings: 10

Ingredients:

7/10 cup almond milk, unsweetened

1 tsp lemon juice

1 1/2 oz. buttermilk

1 medium banana, mashed

1/4 cup maple syrup or 1 tbsp. liquid stevia

1 1/2 tbsp vanilla extract, non-alcoholic

1/4 tbsp. sea salt

3/4 cup all-purpose flour

1/4 tbsp. cinnamon, dried

1 medium rolled oats

3/4 tbsp. baking powder

1/4 tbsp. baking soda

1/2 cup unsweetened chocolate chips

1/4 cup chopped hazelnuts (if desired)

1/5 cup maple syrup (if desired)

1/4 tbsp. cinnamon, ground (if desired)

Directions:

1. Preheat the oven to about 350 deg. F.

2. Add the almond milk and lemon juice to a large mixing bowl, thoroughly whisk to combine, and then set aside about 5 minutes.

3. In another large bowl, add the buttermilk, mashed banana, maple syrup, vanilla extract, and salt to taste.

4. Stir thoroughly the flour, cinnamon, oats, baking powder, and soda in a separate bowl.

5. Transfer the almond milk mixture into the maple syrup mixture, thoroughly whisk to combine, until well incorporated.

6. Whisk in the milk mixture into the flour mixture, thoroughly whisk to combine.

7. Stir in the hazelnuts (if using) and unsweetened chocolate chips.

8. Line up a baking pan with a tin foil or parchment paper or spray with cooking oil, and then pour the mixture onto the pan, leaving spaces.

9. Bake, at 350 deg. F., about 25 minutes, or until a toothpick could come out clean when inserted.

10. Let stand to cool, and then serve, topped with a mixture of dried cinnamon and maple syrup if desired.

Chili Cheese Dip

This creamy hearty dip satisfies your cravings to the fullest. A favorite and hit with guests at the next party.

Preparation Time: 20 minutes

Cooking Time: 20 minutes

Total Time: 40 minutes

Servings: 6

Ingredients:

1/2 medium yellow onion, minced

1 cup raw cashews, soaked for 24 hours, drained

1/2 tsp. nutritional yeast

1 cup almond milk, unsweetened

1 cup balsamic vinegar

1 red bell pepper, roasted, seeded, roughly chopped

1 tbsp. chili powder

1 tbsp. yellow mustard

1/2 tsp. sea salt, or to taste

1 1/2 cups black beans, low sodium drained and rinsed

2 medium salsa, fresh

1 tbsp. chili

1/8 tbsp. granulated garlic,

1/8 tbsp. dried onion,

1/2 tbsp. dried cumin

1/8 tbsp. red pepper flakes

1/8 tbsp. dried oregano

1/8 tbsp. Smokey paprika

1/8 tbsp. ground pepper

1 Package Tortilla chips

Directions:

1. Add some water to a large frying pan, sauté the onion over medium heat, stir repeatedly to avoid sticking, add the black beans, salsa, and seasonings, sauté, stir, about 5 minutes or until flavorful.

2. Meanwhile, add the soaked cashews, yeast, milk, balsamic vinegar, roasted red bell pepper, chili powder, yellow mustard, and salt to a food processor or high powered blender.

3. Transfer the blended sauce into the sautéed vegetable and seasonings, sauté, until heated through. Let stand to cool.

4. Serve, topped with crackers, or any of your favorite toppings.

Cranberry Buttermilk Coconut Bars

Enjoy these perfect and flavorful bars for breakfast. Tasty and delicious!

Preparation Time: 30 minutes

Cooking Time: 30 minutes

Total Time: 1 hour

Servings: 16

Ingredients:

2 and 1/2 cups buttermilk

6 tsp. chia seeds

1 and 1/2 cups old fashioned oats, ground into flour in a blender

1 medium oat, old fashioned

1/2 tbsp. baking powder

1 medium chopped walnut

1 cup cranberries, frozen or fresh

1 cup shredded coconut

1/4 tsp. salt

2/3 cup fruit puree

1/4 cup vegetable shortening

2 tsp. lemon extract

1/3 cup maple syrup

Directions:

1. Preheat the oven to about 350 deg. F., and then line up a baking sheet with an 8 x 8-inch parchment paper or tin foil.

2. Add the buttermilk and chia seeds to a small mixing bowl, thoroughly mix, set aside to thicken.

2. In a separate bowl, add the oat flour, oats, baking powder, walnuts, cranberries, coconut, and salt, thoroughly whisk until well mixed.

3. Whisk in the fruit puree, vegetable shortening, lemon extract, and maple syrup thoroughly until well combined.

4. Press the dough into the pan with a wooden spoon or spatula, bake, at 350 deg. F., about 30 minutes, or until the edges begin to turn brown.

5. Let stand to cool, cut into 16 equal squares.

Vegan Fruits & Seeds Smoothie

Thinking of a good way to begin your day? These fruits & seeds smoothies make a great snack you would not want to resist. Yummy!

Preparation Time: 10 minutes

Total Time: 10 minutes

Servings: 2

Ingredients:

1 stalk celery

1 carrot peeled and roughly chopped

Handful broccoli sprouts (about 1/2 cup)

1 cup cabbage, roughly chopped

1/2 cup parsley

1/2 tomato roughly chopped

1/2 avocado

1 banana, mashed

1/2 green apple

1/2 cup non-dairy milk

2 tsp. chia seeds

2 tsp. flaxseeds

Directions:

1. Add all the ingredients into a food processor or blender, puree, about 2-3 minutes, or until smoothened without lumps.

2. If too thick, you can add a little water.

Puffed Corn with Cinnamon Nut Granola

This low fat puffed corn and cinnamon nut granola are very easy to prepare. Delicious, healthy, and very easy to bake. Yummy!

Preparation Time: 20 minutes

Cooking Time: 30 minutes

Total Time: 50 minutes

Servings: 8

Ingredients:

10 ounces whole oats

10 ounces corn, puffed

10 ounces millet, puffed

1 medium pistachio or sliced almond walnuts

3/4 cup raisins or dried cranberries

2 and 1/2 tbsp. maple syrup

1/2 cup vegetable oil

1 tbsp. Ceylon cinnamon

1/2 tbsp. vanilla extract, non-alcoholic

1/4 tsp. sea salt

Topping:

1/2 cup shredded coconut

Directions:

1. Preheat the oven to about 300 deg. F.

2. Add the whole oats, puffed millet, corn, and pistachios or nuts, raisins or dried cranberries to a large mixing bowl, stir to mix.

3. Add the maple syrup, vegetable oil, vanilla extract, cinnamon, and salt to another separate bowl, thoroughly whisk to combine.

4. Thoroughly whisk in the maple syrup mixture with the cereals mixture to combine perfectly well.

5. Drop large spoonfuls by spreading on 2 parchment paper-lined baking sheets.

6. Bake, at 300 deg. F., about 35 to 45 minutes, turn at 15 minutes intervals until lightly browned. Remove from heat, let sit to cool.

7. Top with shredded coconut, stir and serve instantly.

END

Thank you for reading my book. If you enjoyed it, would you please take a moment to leave me a review at any of your favorite retailers?

Thanks!

Florence Rivers

Printed in Poland
by Amazon Fulfillment
Poland Sp. z o.o., Wrocław